## In Praise of William M. Upson and Steven F. Klamm...

*"Your assistance in the areas of financial planning and meeting long-term insurance needs has proven beneficial for me personally and for the corporation. You have effectively reduced my personal taxes and provided the diversification my pension plan needed to assure long-term growth on a conservative basis."*
 -Edward D. Grieve, V.P. Marketing, United Van Lines

*"Bill Upson has been a life saver for me. When several years ago I received a settlement of money...I went to Bill. [He] made all the difference. Through the years I have been pleased time and again with the choice I made. My family is grateful as well..."* -Betsy Glen, Client

*"I want to thank you...The attendees spoke highly of your presentation on Long-Term Care...Your extensive background and experience was quite evident in the wealth of knowledge that you shared."* -Marshall L. Schield, Schield Management Company

*"I would like to thank you...Our chapter members were impressed and informed by your presentations. Several...remarked...it was the best meeting we had presented in the past twenty years."* -Michael Holman, President, NAIFA-South Puget Sound

*"Over the years, I found that I needed someone I could trust to responsibly handle my personal, business, insurance and estate planning needs. Bill has far exceeded my expectations."* -Jack King, Investor and Client

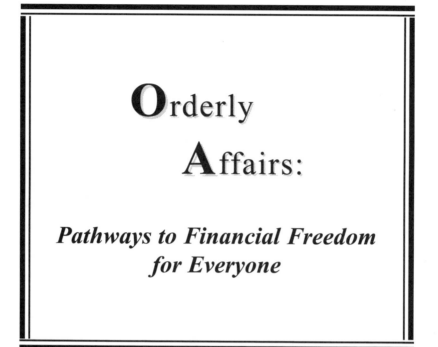

# Orderly Affairs:

## Pathways to Financial Freedom for Everyone

## William M. Upson, CLU, ChFC and Steven F. Klamm, Esq.

St. Bernie's Press
P.O. Box 5558
Walnut Creek, CA 94596

A portion of the profits from this book will go to worthy causes that help our global neighbors learn about financial responsibility, wealth attainment and successful life planning.

ORDERLY AFFAIRS
Pathways to Financial Freedom for Everyone
by
William M. Upson, CLU, ChFC
and Steven F. Klamm, Esq.

Published by: St. Bernie's Press
Post Office Box 5558
Walnut Creek CA 94596
(800) 765-0561
www.strategicasset.net

ISBN 0-9678982-1-8
First Printing 2002

Library Of Congress Control Number: 2002105920

This publication is designed to provide accurate and authoritative information regarding the subject matter covered. It is sold with the understanding that the publisher is not engaged in rendering legal, accounting or other professional service. If legal advice or other expert assistance is required, the services of a competent professional person should be sought.
- From a Declaration of Principles jointly adopted by a Committee of the American Bar Association and a Committee of Publishers and Associations.

Printed in the United States of America

Also by William Upson: *Long-Term Care...Alternatives and Solutions* (St. Bernie's Press, 2000)

To our parents, who showed us the way and gave us truth and love.

# FOREWORD

There are many excellent "how to" books available on the mechanics of financial planning. What we wanted to try and give you, the reader of this book, is something a little different - *inspiration*.

This book provides real-life examples of individuals who have been financially successful and explains how these people obtained that success.

Over the years, we have had the privilege to observe exactly how many of our clients accomplished their financial goals. As their financial advisor, I personally have noted that financially successful individuals have certain characteristics which lead to success. These characteristics are emphasized in the first chapter, but are described throughout the book.

We have tried to illustrate that there are many pathways to achieve financial success. Hopefully, as you read these stories, one or more will strike a chord in you. We intend these cases to serve as an inspiration that will encourage you to create a financial plan - something we strongly believe to be a necessary key to your success.

In the early process of assembling the stories for this book, it became apparent that I was going to need help putting together not only the stories of the individuals themselves, but also describing the "rules of the game", including the financial tools necessary to obtain success. I enlisted the help of my friend and colleague, Steve Klamm. Steve is someone whom I have had the pleasure of working with over the last 13 years. We have many mutual clients at this point, based not only upon his thorough understanding of tax law, trusts and estate planning, but his ability to work with and gain the confidence of clients. Many of the situations described in this book are based upon cases we have worked on together.

Steve and I both feel it is imperative that you have a written plan of attack in order to achieve your financial goals. Before you can do this, however, you also will need a basic understanding of some of the most important financial tools available. Without this understanding, you are not going to be comfortable taking control of your financial destiny. Your ability to take control - at least at some level - of your financial destiny will be the key determinant in how you fare compared to the person who has an understanding of how these tools work.

It was my intention to make this book as entertaining as possible while being informative for you. I hope I have succeeded and that you enjoy, as well as benefit from, the stories in this book.


*Bill Upson*

# ACKNOWLEDGMENTS

Undertaking the writing of a book is truly a "team" effort. Without the contribution of the many talented individuals involved, this work might have languished for months, if not years.

Behind every good writer there is a good editor, and we would like to thank Elly Rabben for her tireless efforts to help shape our fragmented words and ideas into a readable manuscript.

Our production team of Emielle Cody, Sheron Irons and Rich Jacobson provided more than just blood, sweat and tears; their talent, thoughts and ideas can be found throughout this volume.

We would like to thank Ron Silva for his input regarding chapters 8 (Saving for your Children's College Education) and 9 (Annuities). We would also like to thank everyone at Galaxy Press and Consolidated Printing for their efforts to make this a quality product.

Additional invaluable contributions of material and ideas were unfailingly supplied by Janice Kraft, Nanette Conkel, Jennifer Denno, Peter Upson and Jon Wood, CPA, whenever our own well of ideas ran dry.

We count ourselves extremely fortunate to work in professional fields that allow us to be associated with quality individuals as clients. Their own stories of perseverance and achievement continue to inspire us and provide us with ample justification for our efforts.

We also express our sincere appreciation to members of the "Million Dollar Round Table" for their feedback and support throughout the conceptualization of this project.

Above all, however, we wish to express our gratitude to each of our families for their love, guidance and support; without which, none of this could have been possible.

# CONTENTS

INTRODUCTION                                                              1

1    From Zero to a Million                                              5
2    Where to Begin: Savings and Mutual Funds                          15
3    How to Handle Changes in the Financial Markets                    33
4    Unloading Debt and Getting Uncle Sam on Your Side                 39
5    Why Insurance Should be Part of Your Financial Plan               47
6    Home, Sweet Home                                                  59
7    Start Retiring Now                                                65
8    Saving for Your Children's College Education                      73
9    Annuities                                                         83
10   Should You Retire Early?                                          93
     What You Need to Know About Social Security
11   Medicare, Medicaid and Medi-Cal                                   99
12   How to Choose a Financial Advisor                                109
13   Living Trusts                                                    117
14   Charitable Trusts                                                123
15   Other Special Types of Trusts                                    131
16   How to Build a Real Estate Empire                                135
17   Being in Business:  From Getting In to Getting Out               141
18   Employee Stock Ownership Plans                                   151
Appendix A                                                            159
Appendix B                                                            165
Appendix C                                                            169

# *Introduction*

"It *isn't what the book costs; it's what it will cost you if you don't read it.*"

So says Jim Rohn, inspirational speaker and author. He observes that many of us get "rickets of the mind" because we do not read enough good books that can help us to success, however we define that.

The poet Robert Frost speaks about life's decisions in his poem, "The Road Not Taken":

> *Two roads diverged in a wood, and I -*
> *I took the one less traveled by,*
> *And that has made all the difference.*

In making life's choices, many will seek the easy way, hoping that less will be expected of them. At the end of the day, some may even be satisfied with that. A special few, however, will say that the easy way is not enough for them. They will find a better and more fulfilling path because they know in their hearts that, while life can sometimes be hard, it also gives us tremendous opportunities for joy and satisfaction as well as the chance to accomplish extraordinary things.

This very same principle can be applied to making our financial future free from worry. You see, saving is simple; it is the attitude about saving that is the hard part. It is a sad commentary on our time that, despite the great resources and monumental wealth created in the last 50 years, fewer than five people out of every 100 can retire comfortably when they reach this time in their lives. Considering the tremendous number of "Baby Boomers" who will be retiring in the next 10-20 years, our society is now faced with a unique challenge; what changes can we make today to improve our chances of living a dignified and high quality life in the future?

The ancient Roman historian Sallus said, "Every man is the architect of his own fortune". When you decide that you will change your life, you are mapping a course from a known but possibly unsatisfying future to a future that may appear far more uncertain but filled with unlimited opportunities and bounty. This book can help you navigate through some of the uncertainty.

Let's start with an example of what happens with gaining weight. If you were to gain just eight ounces per month this would translate into six pounds per year. At the end of 40 years you would weigh 240 pounds more than you do today! This is an example of what happens when we fail to pay attention to small results that accumulate over long periods of time.

Now, using the same concept, imagine changing a single spending habit that results in you being able to save $3.35 a day. This change, by itself, would result in an annual saving of $1,200. Even with such a modest approach, at the end of 40 years you would have $48,000 plus all the income your investments earned, for a total of about $1,264,000 (before income and capital gains taxes). What a magnificent result for such a small daily adjustment in spending!

What could you forego each day that you now spend $3.35 on? The change in behavior we are talking about amounts to giving up something as insignificant as an extra coffee, a sweet treat, a pack of cigarettes or walking instead of riding somewhere. Making such a choice can not only result in a tremendous accumulation of savings but can also have multiple other benefits on your life such as better health, an attitude of self-reliance and freedom from worrying about your financial future.

Consider this too; the wealth you create during your working years must not only sustain you during your retirement, it must continue to grow if it is to survive you. If recent trends in health and longevity continue, your retirement years may very well be greater than your working years.  Above and beyond the quality of life you may desire to live during your retirement, consider the magnificent estate you might create for the benefit of your heirs or for your favorite school or charity.

"Experience is the best teacher", it is often said, and many times it is the best way to achieve our goals.  As authors of this book, we believe it is important to look at successful individuals as teachers and leaders who can profoundly affect our future happiness and prosperity if we are willing to learn from their experiences.  We also believe that the future successes you may achieve can affect not only your own life and family's happiness, but also an entire community, city or even an entire culture positively.  As the world in which we live grows smaller daily, we find more and more that the actions we take and the choices we make can have a very profound effect on people the world over.

If you can dream and visualize objectives that will be the focus of your life then you have the power to get through the tough times when it might seem impossible to move forward.  Most of us desire material gain, freedom from worry, and a chance to grow mentally, spiritually, or emotionally.  Sometimes these goals can only be achieved by stepping away from old thought patterns and habits that got us into a rut in the first place.

Through the stories of other people's experiences, this book will give you the tools and the knowledge to increase your financial well being, plan a more secure future, and, we hope, allow you to someday give back to society.  Some of these stories are about overcoming incredible hardships, limited education, physical limitations, and yet succeeding in spite of the improbable odds.  Some of the stories are about doing a very simple thing extraordinarily well, and achieving success and freedom from life's vagaries.  Some of the stories are about very average people who never aspired to great fortunes or magnificent achievements but who have truly touched thousands of people by their generosity and good works.

In reading the compelling stories that follow, you will learn how individuals achieved remarkable success simply by paying attention to the critical "little" day-to-day choices they faced and choosing, invariably, the one that would lead them to their long-term goals. The Chinese philosopher Lao-Tsu said it so clearly hundreds of years ago: "A journey of a thousand miles must begin with a single step". What is your first step? This book can show you. It can help you transform your life into one of rich reward and great promise. We sincerely hope this book will inspire you to take action in your life so that you may achieve the future you are capable of and deserve.

# *From Zero to a Million*

*"Our business is not to get rich quickly; if you do the right things right, you can get rich slowly."*
- Burton L. Herman

MADELINE

Madeline was still a child when her father was killed in an industrial accident, leaving her family virtually destitute. They were within days of being put out on the street when a family friend came forward and helped them stay in their home. Still, it was a life with only the bare necessities.

As soon as Madeline was old enough to go to work, she found a job as a telephone operator. She never married and never made more than $20,000 a year in all the time she worked, but the memory of her family's financial struggle during childhood gave her the drive she needed to secure her financial future. This experience also gave Madeline a strong desire to help others in difficult circumstances.

Over the years, Madeline was offered stock by the phone company, which she gladly accepted. She also bought single shares when she had the money, never more than $100 at a time, the most she could afford. And she saved.

At age 73, her total retirement income, including Social Security, was $25,000 a year. Of this, she paid income taxes of about $5,000. Despite her small income, Madeline believed deeply in giving to charity and sent donations of $5 to $50 to more than 50 charities around the world each year.

By this point in her life, Madeline had managed to grow her savings into $200,000 in investments, including $150,000 of phone company stock accumulated in the 50 years she worked. She lived a life that was frugal but, by her own definition, was comfortable and allowed her to travel the world, spend time with friends and family, fish and walk the beaches she loved near where she lived.

Eventually, Madeline realized that she might be able to do more with her money if she sought professional advice. In 1990 she asked a professional financial advisor (and longtime family friend) to take over her investment accounts. She wanted not only to keep her money growing, but also to minimize her taxes and provide money to fund her desire for philanthropy.

To increase her returns and decrease her taxes, the advisor recommended that she invest some of her money in annuity contracts (explained in a later chapter). This completely avoided current taxes, left more "after-tax" dollars to invest and allowed her investment accounts to grow much faster. Despite her age, the advisor also suggested she purchase life insurance as a way to provide her intended heirs with a sizeable benefit in the event of her death.

*A Change in Circumstances*

By 1995 Madeline was having difficulty managing her own affairs and she asked her advisor to take charge of all her financial matters. Her assets had grown considerably, and now a living trust was in order. Her will was also reviewed and it was discovered that the executor she had named earlier had died. A new executor was named.

The advisor also wanted Madeline to purchase long-term care insurance coverage. Unfortunately, her health had already deteriorated to the point where she could no longer qualify for this type of insurance.

In 1997, her financial position was re-evaluated. Additional planning led to the creation of a charitable trust. This trust was funded with phone company stock that had appreciated from a cost of $10,000 to a current value over $100,000. This type of trust provided substantial tax benefits that she could utilize during her lifetime, greatly reducing Madeline's income taxes for an extended period of years. Additionally, she would also receive income from the trust for the balance of her life. At her death the trust principal would transfer to the charitable beneficiaries she had named free of all income and estate taxes.

Upon further review, her advisor also found that some of Madeline's phone company stock was now losing value. Changes were made to more productive investments, and her portfolio was professionally diversified.

By the late 1990s, Madeline's health had seriously deteriorated. She had fallen and broken bones several times. It was recommended that she consider moving into a retirement center and she reluctantly agreed to move and sell her home. That decision, while emotionally difficult, freed up considerable equity she had gained through appreciation in the value of her house over the years. This money provided for more suitable accommodations without having to draw upon her investment funds. It also meant that, after her death, her estate could be closed without a great deal of delay.

In 2000, Madeline died, leaving an estate valued at $1.1 million; her legacy of over 50 years of hard work and careful money management. In keeping with her lifelong desire, all of her money was given to seven charities. The living trust, the charitable trust, and the other planning completed prior to her death allowed 100% of the assets to pass to the charities with no capital gains, income or estate taxes.

As a result of her penchant for living within her means, paying herself first by disciplined savings and through professional money management, there are now endowments, bequests, grants and scholarships to young men and women in her community that did not previously exist. Although she never had children of her own, Madeline has touched generations of young people with her generosity and she has helped change the focus of an entire community's outreach program dedicated to those in need. The impact that this incredible woman had on her community, amplified through careful planning, was and continues to be very dramatic.

*How did Madeline do it?*

- Disciplined investment over a long period of time.

- Buying stock whenever she could in whatever amount she could.

- Paying attention to the effect of income and capital gains taxes on her net income.

- Getting the advice of professional advisors, including legal, accounting, banking, real estate and financial advisors, which maximized the return on her investments and minimized her taxes.

- Creating a working financial plan that met her needs and could be adjusted as those needs changed.

- Having a clear vision of what she wanted to do; focusing on her own financial well being as well as that of her community.

By maintaining a clear picture in her mind of what she wanted to achieve and utilizing the assistance of individuals who could get her there, Madeline was able to move decisively to make her vision a lasting reality. As we shall see in the stories to come, having discipline, a clear vision of your future and getting the support and assistance of people who can help you make this a reality, are the cornerstones to financial success.

JORGE

Madeline isn't the only person who started with nothing and built a comfortable life. Another example is Jorge, who grew up poor in a foreign country. At a young age, he decided that he wanted to be an auto mechanic. When he was old enough, his determination to become a mechanic resulted in Jorge being accepted by training schools for several car manufacturers in Europe. After he finished his training, he traveled to the United States, eventually settling in the San Francisco bay area.

Jorge would frequently drive by the expensive homes in the hills surrounding the bay area and see two, three and four cars parked in the driveways. Unlike many people who merely dream about owning one of the expensive houses on the hill, Jorge saw an opportunity. He reasoned that people would dearly love to have their luxury automobiles cared for by an expert who looked after their cars better than they could themselves. It became his goal to provide this extraordinary level of service at a reasonable price that dealerships could not offer at the time.

After working for auto repair shops for a few years and setting aside money, he decided to start his own business. He opened a full-service auto repair business specializing in superior service. Over the years, his quality of service and attention to detail earned him an unsurpassed reputation. Word of mouth resulted in a continuously growing list of loyal clients with all types of cars needing his special care, and willing to pay for premium service. His aspiration, along with his drive and enthusiasm, set him down the path to become one of the very best mechanics in the bay area servicing luxury automobiles.

Note that even though Jorge wanted to own one of the homes on the hill, he knew that he would first have to build a business that would provide the income to achieve his goal. By having the discipline to build a successful business first he was able to realize his ultimate goal of a luxury house on the hill.

Jorge did not solely limit his focus to the auto service business. With an eye to the future, he set up a retirement plan and he made regular deposits into it. He also maintained adequate forms of insurance, including life, disability, medical and general liability insurance. This ensured that he and his family would be provided for in the event of some unknown disaster or illness that might befall them.

In time, Jorge grew weary of the day-to-day stress of running a busy shop and he sold the business to one of his employees. Under the buyout terms he negotiated, he drew an on-going income from the business.

Jorge also had the foresight to see the potential future value of the land on which his shop was located. Over the years he bought not only the building that housed his former business, but also the real estate around it. Now he receives a five-figure monthly income for rent from the property he was wise enough to buy years earlier.

With the income from the sale of his business, his real estate income and Social Security, Jorge was able to retire comfortably with a diverse and secure portfolio. Funds moved from his profit-sharing plan to his IRA continue to grow tax-deferred until he must take required minimum distributions (RMDs) beginning at age 70 1/2.

CHRISTOPHER

Christopher came from a middle class family of four children. When he was 15, his sister died and this so affected him that he decided to leave home and school. At the time, full of youthful innocence and bravado, he claimed he was either going to be a bum on the street or a millionaire. Secretly, in his heart, Christopher was convinced that he could one day become a multi-millionaire.

He went out and got a specialized job in construction and learned how to improve water systems located in apartment houses, condominiums and hotels. Christopher worked long and hard to learn the specialized needs of his customers. Consequently, the company grew rapidly and the owner eventually gave him a 20%

interest in the company in recognition of his efforts.

It soon became apparent to Christopher that the 80% partner needed Christopher far more than Christopher needed him. His partner was busy spending so much time and money traveling around the world "playing" that he was neglecting the basic operation of the company. These divisions were putting the entire operation at risk.

Christopher worked harder and harder to save the company, but eventually realized that it just wouldn't be possible. He then negotiated with his partner to trade his 20% ownership interest in exchange for three major clients that he could take with him to his own company. His partner agreed to this settlement, launching Christopher toward his own very successful company.

Before he started his own company, however, Christopher spent many months preparing. He spent time listening to engineers and construction people talk about the work that they did and how they did it. All of his research was done after hours, at the end of a long day's labor when the desire for a little rest and relaxation was extremely tempting. Although Christopher could have taken the easy path, he chose instead to keep his goal of starting his own company first and foremost in his mind. This allowed him to learn from the experiences of others and one day be able to do it himself.

By the time he started his business, Christopher had mastered the basics so that his clients were more than satisfied with him and his services. Now, at 34 years of age, he makes a six-figure income and has 16 people working for him. Christopher recently hired a business manager from one of the big telecommunications companies to run his business for him. Even to this day, while on vacation or traveling, Christopher seeks opportunities for his business. As a consequence, he is now beginning to build an international business.

Despite his success, Christopher remains committed to the values that got him where he is and to his roots. Upon the passing of his parents, Christopher bought the family residence and renovated it to meet his needs. He could afford a large house in a new development, but he preferred to stay right in the same neighborhood where he grew up (a very common trait with self-made millionaires). Although he never did go back to school, through his ingenuity and hard work Christopher is well on his way to becoming very successful, ensuring all of his future needs will met.

Here are some of the key points that represent what these individuals' lives illustrate for all of us:

- Have a clear vision of your financial and personal goals.

- Have the discipline to match your daily activities to achieving those goals.

- Be willing to seek professional advice including investment, banking, real estate and legal, as needed.

- Create a working written financial plan or "road map" that meets your needs and can be adjusted as those needs change.

One of the best ways to ensure that your financial future will hold all the comfort and security you desire is to learn the "short-cuts" that have taken others many years to realize. In the next chapter, we'll begin to explore the amazing value and effectiveness of these "financial power tools".

# *Where to Begin: Savings and Mutual Funds*

*"Most people have it all wrong about wealth in America. Wealth is not the same as income. If you make a good income each year and spend it all, you are not getting wealthier. You are just living high. Wealth is what you accumulate, not what you spend."*

- Thomas Stanley and William D. Danko
in "The Millionaire Next Door."

Most of us live up to the limit of our income, and perhaps beyond. Consumer debt in this country is at an all-time high, while savings rates are at historic lows. Many can barely scrape together the money to pay their bills each month. For many people, it seems impossible to squeeze out even a penny to put away for savings, even though they know they should.

Perhaps they are young. The idea of retirement to a young person in their twenties, thirties or even forties may seem ridiculously far off into the future. Encouraged by our "instant gratification" society, they believe there's no time like the present to have fun and spend money. In fact, the advertising industry has known this for years and has mainly pitched anything to do with travel, partying (alcohol and entertainment), clothes and cars to the demographically prime target of the twenty to thirty-something age bracket. In almost every respect, our society reinforces this view that youth is a time to enjoy the relative lack of responsibility, "hang loose" and not think about tomorrow.

# The Power of Money and Time

| | \$1000 to start and \$100/month invested over* | | | |
|---|---|---|---|---|
| | **10yrs** | **20yrs** | **30yrs** | **40yrs** |
| **Total Amount Invested** | \$12,900 | \$24,900 | \$36,900 | \$48,900 |
| **Amount at End of Period** | \$24,446 | \$129,797 | \$509,008 | \$1,366,663 |

*Returns based on the performance of an "average" mutual fund over the time period

The best time to start planning for financial security, however, is exactly when time is on your side. The earlier you begin, the less money it takes to reach the same goal and the more time you have to recover from unavoidable reverses.

Often, finding the money to save means changing long-ingrained habits, a difficult challenge for most of us. Just like losing weight, the easiest way to change a habit is to start small.

Many people ignore the effect that small daily expenditures can have on their annual and lifetime budget. Adding up coffees, newspapers, snacks, meals out, after work drinks, unplanned dining out, discarding loose change into "tip" jars and other "dollar-a-day" expenses can, at the end of the year, amount to thousands of dollars. Ask yourself: do you really need to eat out every weekday? If you packed your lunch only one day a week, you could save $25 to $50 a month, or almost $600 a year. That's like giving yourself an $800 or $900 raise before tax!

Note that we are not talking about a complete end to fun and spontaneity. Our point is, rather, that spending should be done consciously, whatever the goal or motive. All too often, spending is, like unhealthy eating, a reflection of unconscious and compulsive behavior that compromises long-term well-being for the benefit of instant gratification. Americans often spend outrageous amounts on exercise equipment and diet programs when a much less expensive and far more effective "program" of healthy eating and physical activity would have sufficed. The same choices that can and do support a healthy lifestyle also serve the goal of reducing daily indulgences that drain your wallet and compromise your long-term financial security.

Why not buy a bag of fruit and keep it at your desk? Walk instead of jumping into the car for short distances. Take the stairs instead of the elevator. Share these ideas with your co-workers. You may find you'll have company and support in making these changes and you'll all be eating more healthfully, losing weight naturally, and you can all put the money you save in the bank.

For those who love the latest technological gadgets ask yourself: do I really need the latest electronic toy? Not only will the newest technology have bugs that older models most likely won't have, but the newest doodad on the market will cost you far, far more. Instead, buy items that are just behind "the curve". You'll save anywhere from 30% to 60% of the cost of the latest technology. If you must have a new feature, see if you can wait six months. As sure as the sun will rise, if you wait just a little, the price of the equipment will come down.

Do you use your cell phone to chat with friends on impulse during the day? Notice how those pennies per minute add up to serious dollars on your monthly statement? You can save a lot of money over the course of a year if you wait until you get home in the evening to make those calls or see if you can change to a cheaper calling plan.

You also may be one of the fortunate few who have money left over to save but never get around to depositing it into your savings account. Have those savings automatically deducted from your paycheck and deposited into an IRA account or a conservative mutual fund where you can't tap it without a penalty. Again, at the end of the year you will be amazed and proud about how much money has accumulated for your future.

Do you have so many debts that you don't know what to pay first? This is a topic we'll explore in much greater detail in a later chapter, but for now consider paying down debt. First and foremost, start with high interest, non-tax-deductible credit card debt. Again, be sure to put that money aside into savings.

Are you an impulse shopper? This is a problem faced by millions of Americans. In fact, one of the greatest threats to your financial well-being is taking advantage of all those "pre-approved" credit card offers. The average person has about six credit cards - far more than what is needed and all designed to tempt you to spend on impulse. Your life will be much simpler and easier if you try keeping just one or two of the most widely accepted cards.

Another time-tested technique is to pay for consumer items with cash or debit cards where the "pain" of spending is most likely to keep your impulses in check. If you want to buy yourself a present, why not keep it small and set a limit that matches your budget? When you see an item you think you just must have, take it off the shelf and carry it around the store as you look at other things. You may find that you reconsider your purchase before taking it home. Those who love to indulge themselves with designer clothes and shoes can save a lot of money without sacrificing their wardrobe by avoiding expensive boutiques and seeking out your favorite brands' factory outlet stores.

These tips individually can save you significant amounts of money. Taken together, however, they add up to very substantial amounts on a monthly or yearly basis. Keep in mind, as well, that time and the miracle of compound growth on your savings will produce results much greater and faster than you can imagine.

To illustrate the powerful effect that savings, investment and lifestyle choices can have on your financial future, consider the following story.

## PAULA and ROBERT

Paula and Robert are old college friends. Over the years, however, they have developed very different lifestyles. Both are 35 years old and make comfortable salaries. When Paula was growing up, her parents gave her money for whatever she needed -- or wanted. Now that she has her own income, she has purchased on credit a high-powered sports car, goes skiing most weekends, plus she spends two weeks a year at a high-end resort in Aspen, Colorado. She also rents a luxury apartment and just bought three rooms full of new furniture - on credit. She uses credit cards for everything: lunch, gas, clothes and vacations. She tells her friends it's "so I can track my expenses better". When the credit card bills come in, however, she often finds she is short on cash to cover her minimum payments, and she panics.

Paula feels nervous and guilty about her spending habits but doesn't know how to live the life she wants to live without going into debt. Lately, she has started to get cash advances on some cards to pay others. She doesn't like the situation but blames her job and insufficient pay for not being able to keep up. Retirement is still 30 years away, she tells herself. She has plenty of time to think about saving later, or so she thinks.

Robert, on the other hand, comes from a family where everyone was expected to contribute financially. He had an after-school job even as a teenager. He was allowed to spend only part of his money on himself. Some of it went into the family "pot," which was always invested. Now that he is on his own, he has continued the habit of setting aside some money each month for the future. He started with $5,000 when he was only 25, putting it into a mutual fund. He figures he can continue putting in $5,000 each year and can average 10% growth over time.

At the end of the first year he had $5,524. After ten years, his "pot" had grown to more than $90,000! Twenty years from now, by the time he is 55, even if he puts nothing more into the account, his investment will have grown to $728,000! If Robert continues to fund his investment account at the same rate until he reaches 55, the total will grow to over $900,000!

Paula knows about Robert's growing stash of money and feels inspired by it. She thinks she could squeeze out $7,500 a year in savings if she could just unload her credit card debt. What she doesn't know is that even if she saves $7,500 a year for 20 years

## Paula & Robert's Retirement Savings at Age 55

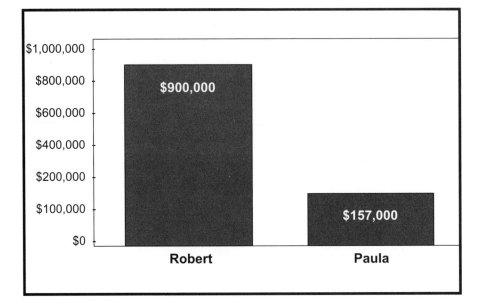

(compared to Robert's $5,000 a year for ten years), she will still have only $157,000 compared to his almost three-quarters of a million dollars, at the same 10% rate of return.

Why? The difference is the length of time Robert gained by starting earlier and the ability of the "magic of compound interest" to turn modest amounts into huge sums if given enough time.

Will Paula be prepared for retirement, even with another ten years of saving and investing? Not likely. A survey of the baby boom generation by a large financial firm revealed that, on average, only $120,000 had been put away toward retirement, which was, in most cases, ten to 15 years into the future. The individuals surveyed had estimated they would need a minimum of $30,000 a year to live on in retirement, and yet they had not taken any time to consider where that $30,000 would come from.

Most, if not all, are counting on the fact that Social Security will bail them out in their retirement years. As we move further forward in time, however, the likelihood of Social Security being the "security blanket" it is today will decrease dramatically, as will all benefits and services provided by government. To have an income of $30,000 a year in today's dollars, a 45 year-old would need about $1 million in retirement savings, assuming an 8% return and 4% inflation!

The bottom line? Even a small amount set aside now can pay big dividends over the years. Over time, it has been proven that money for retirement grows much faster by investing in diversified investment accounts. For small investors, mutual funds are often the option of choice, and this is where we now turn.

*What is a Mutual Fund?*

Since their emergence 40 years ago, mutual funds have come to represent the investment option preferred by many Americans. Today, there are more than 10,000 mutual funds in which to invest. Even after 40 years, however, many people still don't understand how a mutual fund works.

A mutual fund is operated by an investment company, which raises money from shareholders (you) and invests it in stocks, bonds, options, futures, currencies or money market securities. In other words, it diversifies your investment, which vastly reduces your risk. Mutual funds, however, vary widely in their investment strategies. Some are low-risk with their money invested in lower-return securities, while some are invested in aggressive high-risk securities with a greater tendency toward high volatility ("ups and downs") over time. There is a wider range of returns from these aggressive funds, with the hope of a higher overall rate of return in the long run. The majority are spread somewhere between this spectrum.

Mutual Funds provide you with professional management of your money, for which you pay a small fee. You may purchase shares in a mutual fund directly from the fund company, getting it as a "no-load" fund.

"If you go through a broker, it is a load fund" may be a true statement in a sense. Today, however, brokers are allowed to provide no-load mutual funds on a fee basis, which may also include other investment advisory services. You need to consider whether you have the time and ability to watch developments in the market and move your money from an under-performing mutual fund to one that has better potential or one that better reflects sectors of the economy that are in favor. Ultimately, you may wish to have a professional manage your funds and make the necessary changes to your investment portfolio over time.

When you invest in mutual funds, you also need to assess your personal tolerance for risk and need for growth. But here's some food for thought: it's tempting to go for aggressive funds because of the potential for high return. Sooner or later, however, such funds will have a setback, possibly very large. If you start with $100,000 and you were to choose between two funds, one with high potential returns but also periodic negative performance versus a conservative fund that plods along with moderate annual growth each year, which would offer you the best overall return?

| Year Fund | Aggressive Fund | | Moderate | |
|---|---|---|---|---|
| | Gain (%) | End Value | Gain (%) | End Value |
| 1 | 20% | $120,000 | 8% | $108,000 |
| 2 | 21% | $145,200 | 8% | $116,640 |
| 3 | 10% | $159,720 | 8% | $125,971 |
| 4 | 16% loss | $134,165 | 8% | $136,049 |
| 5 | 10% | $147,581 | 8% | $146,933 |

Surprise, they're tied! So if you think you can't tolerate a loss like that shown in year four, you can opt for the lower but steadier, return of a conservative fund and be quite comfortable reaching your goal.

The previous example also illustrates the impact that volatility can have on your portfolio performance. It takes a far greater percentage gain to overcome the affect of a particular loss. For instance, a 25% decline in a fund would require a 33% gain just to get back to even. Even more dramatically, a 50% reduction in a fund requires a 100% gain to offset the loss. Thus, the effect of volatility on your investments is much more than a comfort issue- it has real implications for the return you might expect to realize over a given time period. That is why it is so crucial to invest for the long-term, particularly if you are adopting an aggressive strategy.

# The Law of Losing

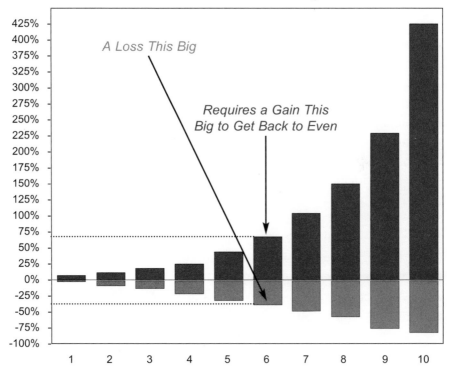

*The Power of Diversity*

Some investors may choose to buy stock directly, rather than using a mutual fund. They may believe that they can spot a "hot" stock or perhaps they have received stock from an employer, such as in a retirement 401(k) account. If a stock is strong, with stable or increasing earnings and an increasing market price, investors may buy as many shares as they can afford and they feel sure of their strategy. But should they?

DANIEL and MEG

Daniel and Meg, in their mid-50s, were concerned about the fact that they had fully three-quarters of their investments in a single stock. At the time, the stock was valued at $90 a share and they had realized a very handsome return on their investment. If they sold off a substantial portion of it, they would suffer a large capital gains tax hit, but if they kept it and the stock plunged, they would have a substantial loss. What should they do?

Their financial advisor recommended that they set up a charitable trust and place the stock inside the trust (discussed in greater detail in the chapter "Charitable Trusts"). Then they could sell their stock with no immediate capital gains tax, a substantial tax deduction, and also have an income from the trust for the rest of their lives. This seemed an ideal strategy for them since they were considering an early retirement.

It was also recommended they purchase a variable annuity contract (described in more detail later on) with the remaining funds they had to invest, in order to realize tax-deferred diversified growth and the ability to let their funds grow tax-free until retirement when they could take them, presumably at a lower income tax rate.

The net result? Daniel and Meg would be able to move funds out of their stock investment, thereby lessening their exposure to future downturns. Their tax liability would be kept to a minimum, resulting in more disposable income to live on than they otherwise would have had. This strategy would reduce risk, achieve diversification and obtain tax-deferred growth through the annuities and charitable trust utilized.

# One Time $100,000 Investment

| Investment | % Return | 20 Years |
|---|---|---|
| $100,000 | 5% | $265,329 |

# VS.

# Five $20,000 Investments
## Earning Different Rates of Return

| Investment | % Return | 20 Years |
|---|---|---|
| $20,000 | 100% loss | $0 |
| $20,000 | 0% | $20,000 |
| $20,000 | 5% | $53,066 |
| $20,000 | 10% | $134,549 |
| $20,000 | 15% | $327,331 |
| $100,000 | | $534,946 |

Unfortunately, they decided not to heed this advice. Thinking that the bull market that was boosting their stock price would continue, they elected to "stand pat" with all their eggs in one very lop-sided basket. They did buy a variable annuity, but not the type recommended, however. When the bull market began to collapse they watched in horror as the price of their shares dropped from $90 to $13 in less than six months. They then both had to go back to work full-time so they could still, hopefully, afford to retire- one day.

Being human, we all think we can "read the tea leaves" when things are going well. Most Americans rate themselves "above average" in investing ability when, by definition, at least half must be below average. It all goes to show that lack of diversification can have a tremendous effect on our long-term investment performance. For this reason alone, the value of an objective outside observer, such as an experienced financial advisor, can be invaluable in keeping you from making this all-too-common mistake.

The chart above graphically illustrates how diversity can save the day. If one hundred thousand dollars is invested in 5 different investments of $20,000 each, even the entire loss of one of the investments and a zero return over twenty years for another doesn't prevent this diversified portfolio from achieving very handsome results when compared to a low-risk, low-return investment of the entire one hundred thousand dollars.

If you still need convincing on the value of diversification in a portfolio, here's another example. Below you will find a comparison between a popular mutual fund and a well-known stock that has been traditionally strong for decades and is a blue chip bellwether of the U.S. economy.

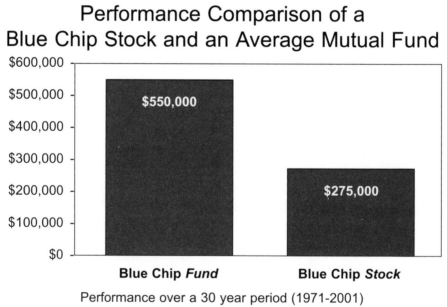

## Performance Comparison of a Blue Chip Stock and an Average Mutual Fund

Performance over a 30 year period (1971-2001)
($1000 initial investment)

Again, you can see from the previous diagram that the inherent strength of a mutual fund is that it can offer superior performance compared to a single stock while reducing overall volatility. The bottom line is that if you have properly diversified your portfolio among many credible companies or securities, in different sectors of the economy, the effect of a single disastrous event on your portfolio can be minimized.

*Other Ways to "Invest"*

Putting money into investments isn't the only thing to consider. It is critical to understand how your income is taxed. Most people look at their overall tax rate, if they think about taxes at all. What they need to focus on, however, is their marginal tax rate. That is, the tax paid on the last few thousand dollars of your income as compared to your total income.

For example, have you had a raise lately? Did you net as much as you expected after taxes from that raise? Probably not. The reason is because our federal tax system is progressive, the more income you make the higher the tax rate on that last bit of income compared to the rate you were paying at your lower earnings level. This higher rate of tax, however, is applied only on the "extra" income earned, and not on your entire earnings. This is often a point of confusion for individuals who believe they'd be better off without a raise because it would put them in a higher tax bracket.

If you add up all the taxes you are paying (federal, state, Social Security and Medicare) and you are single, any income you make between $26,000 and $36,000 is taxed at a whopping 42%. But wait, it gets worse. This does not include state and local sales taxes on your purchases. In fact, the IRS reports that total individual income tax collections have risen four-fold since 1980! (See the next diagram for dramatic proof.)

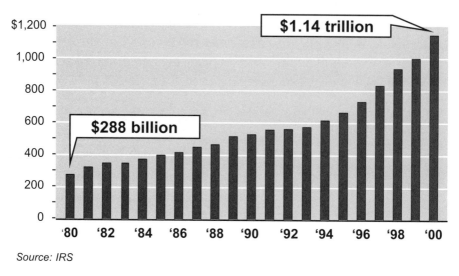

# The Growth of Taxation

$1,200

1,000

800

600

**$1.14 trillion**

**$288 billion**

400

200

0

'80   '82   '84   '86   '88   '90   '92   '94   '96   '98   '00

*Source: IRS*

*The Other Tax to be Aware of - "The Stealth Tax" (Alternative Minimum Tax - AMT)*

Due to inflation, most Americans' overall income goes up over the years, and as it increases it causes the alternative minimum tax to come into effect. This is a tax parallel to the income tax system. Many people are totally unaware of the effects of the AMT on their overall income tax liability yearly. It is currently estimated by the Treasury Department that by 2010, over 35 million taxpayers will be affected by the AMT, and these are people with incomes of $70,000 per year or more, two to three children, a house, and no other significant write-offs. As a consequence, this tax is likely to affect more and more people in the years ahead.

There is no plan currently to do away with the individual AMT, and with government expenses like Medicare and Social Security dependent on this tax for funding there is no expectation of it going away any time soon. So as you look at your income tax, alternative minimum tax and capital gains tax liabilities, it becomes essential that you have the advice of competent financial professionals who can review these taxes on an ongoing basis and advise you on the best long-term strategy for avoiding or reducing AMT.

Other tax saving strategies to be considered include sheltering income from taxes as much as possible. You can do this by socking it away in your company's 401(k) plan or an IRA. Another important tax strategy in the United States is buying a home with debt financing because the money you spend on mortgage interest and property taxes is mostly tax-deductible if you itemize. This reduces the net cost of owning a home by the amount of taxes you would have had to pay if you didn't avail yourself of this generous tax avoidance benefit, courtesy of Uncle Sam.

Remember, too, that over time your 401(k), IRA and real estate investments should increase in value. The average annual growth in residential real estate over the last 160 years has been 5%, annually compounded. That is a rock-solid proven investment that should be part of everyone's investment and tax-planning strategy. If you are renting, only the landlord's investment is growing. Perhaps it's time to take a long, hard look at where your money goes, and start making it work harder for you.

At this point, you are encouraged to begin taking concrete steps toward changing the way you look at your financial challenges and opportunities. Appendix "C" has been provided to help you begin working through this process. We invite you to, now, take some time and examine the questions in this appendix as a way of enhancing the value of the chapters to follow.

# Orderly Affairs

# How to Handle Changes in the Financial Markets

*"The way I see it, if you want the rainbow, you gotta put up with the rain."*

— Dolly Parton

There is one very good reason people used to keep their savings in their mattresses; they had absolute control over what happened to their money.  In an era of poor economic growth, low returns on investment and instability, this may have been a wise strategy.  What they did not have, though, was the ability to help their money grow, nor could they have a hand in strengthening the financial fabric of America.

Investing in corporate America provides those opportunities.  Your investment can increase in value simply by virtue of a company's increasing profits.   In addition, the sale of stock to the public provides companies with money to fund research and development of new products, to expand into new markets or to modernize in order to better compete.

All of this comes at a certain price to the investor: uncertainty.  An investor has no control over whether the financial markets go up or down, and this unpredictability makes many investors very nervous about erosion of their investments.

And so they should be.  It has been shown time and time again that the wealthiest individuals rarely got there by taking unnecessary risk with their capital.   In fact, Warren Buffet, one of America's wealthiest individuals and most famous investors, avoided the "Dot Com" mania (and later meltdown) amid much criticism for his conservative approach.  Now, of course, those same critics applaud his "value" approach to investing.

If there were a mantra for nervous investors, it would be "invest for the long term".  This is because while markets can plunge frighteningly at any time, they eventually recover.  Thus, while bear markets (in which prices fall, usually on bad economic news) reduce your invested capital, they will more than recoup those losses as long as the companies are solid and you remain invested for the inevitable turnaround (based on past historical results and assuming proper diversification and adequate investment horizons).

This is not to imply that every stock will recover. Not every company is well run and those that are managed inefficiently or which are based on a weak market plan may not survive an economic downturn. Still, there are ways to protect yourself -- and your investments. Here are some suggestions:

- Find a competent professional investment advisor. Follow his or her advice, unless you believe he/she does not understand what it is you are trying to accomplish. A written financial plan that is reviewed regularly with that advisor ensures that you are both "on the same page".

- Diversify your holdings so that you are not investing heavily in any one stock or even one sector of the economy (in case that sector is disproportionately affected by some disaster).

- Invest smaller fixed dollar amounts regularly over an extended period of time instead of making a single, large one-time investment. This strategy, called "dollar cost averaging", will ensure you buy less amounts of a stock or mutual fund that is high priced and more when the price is reduced- thereby resulting in a lower average aquisition cost. It also allows you to monitor a company's performance and stop further investments if problems begin to become apparent.

- Monitor investment performance, at least twice a year.

- Meet with your advisor at least annually to review your plan.

Let's consider, for a moment, some historical reasons why some people chose not to invest in the stock market. The following lists some of the calamitous events that have taken place over the last seventy years.

| | | | |
|---|---|---|---|
| 1934 | Depression | 1935 | Spanish Civil War |
| 1936 | Recession | 1937 | War in Europe |
| 1938 | France falls | 1939 | Pearl Harbor |
| 1942 | Wartime price controls | 1944 | Consumer goods shortages |
| 1946 | Dow tops 200: market too high | 1947 | Cold War begins |
| 1948 | Berlin blockade | 1949 | Russia explodes A-bomb |
| 1950 | Korean War | 1951 | Excess Profits tax |
| 1953 | Russia explodes H-bomb | 1954 | Dow tops 300: too high |
| 1956 | Suez crisis | 1958 | Recession |
| 1959 | Castro seizes power in Cuba | 1960 | Russia downs U-2 plane |
| 1961 | Berlin Wall erected | 1962 | Cuban missile crisis |
| 1963 | Kennedy assassinated | 1965 | Civil Rights marches |
| 1966 | Vietnam War escalates | 1967 | Race riots |
| 1968 | USSR Pueblo seized | 1970 | Cambodia invaded: war |
| 1971 | Wage price freeze | 1973 | Energy crisis - gas lines |
| 1974 | Steepest market drop in 4 decades | 1978 | Interest rates rise |
| 1979 | Oil prices skyrocket | 1980 | Interest rates all-time high |
| 1981 | Steep recession begins | 1982 | Worst recession in 40 years |
| 1984 | Record federal deficits | 1986 | Dow near 2000 |
| 1987 | Record-setting market decline | 1988 | Iran hostage crisis |
| 1989 | October "mini-crash" | 1990 | Persian Gulf crisis |
| 1992 | Global recession | 1994 | Interest rates raised 6X |
| 1995 | Dow tops 5,000 | 1997 | Hong Kong reverts to China |
| 1998 | Asian Flu | 1999 | Y2K scare |
| 2000 | Technology bubble burst | 2001 | Terrorist attack on America |
| 2002+ | ?????? | | |

In fact, it is almost guaranteed that in the next ten years there will be some crisis, of one sort or another, that will result in a substantial stock market plunge. <u>Then consider that $10,000 invested in the Standard & Poor 500 Index in January of 1934 would, in 2001, be worth $20,670,000</u>!

The same $10,000 kept in a mattress from 1934 through 2001 would still be worth $10,000.

# Orderly Affairs

# *Unloading Debt and Getting Uncle Sam On Your Side*

*"Our incomes are like our shoes: if too small, they gall and pinch us; but if too large, they cause us to stumble and to trip."*
                                        - Charles C. Colton

S etting money aside each month is only one way to increase your net worth. Another way is to pay down debt over time. Still another is to get rid of charges that you don't absolutely have to pay, such as private mortgage insurance. Paying attention to your tax burden is also an excellent way to add to the bottom line.

The solution to increasing net worth isn't always obvious. One person who considered applying extra funds to pay down his 30-year mortgage over a shorter period of time discovered, upon further analysis, that prepayment of this debt wasn't the most productive use of his money. It takes some investigation to determine why this is so, and for this we turn to the following story.

DON

Don owned his own business, which paid him a substantial income. He had just finished building a new house and he had some extra money but was uncertain whether to use it to pay down his mortgage or to invest it. The house, which was valued at $700,000 at that time, had a mortgage of $350,000.

Don decided that his goal was simply to earn the greatest return on his money, whether by cutting taxes, paying more principal monthly, continuing to pay interest on his mortgage or by investing it for growth.

Let's do an analysis comparing the ten-year performance of the same amount of money invested in a typical portfolio of growth mutual funds versus using that money to pay down Don's mortgage.

What Don found was that assuming the investment portfolio had an average rate of return of 10% (the average achieved by growth funds over the last ten years), it would increase in value by over $550,000. Over the same time period, Don's house would appreciate in value somewhere between $200,000 and $500,000. In both cases, we are assuming rates of return based on prior performance of representative mutual funds and the real estate market in the area where the house was built.

By paying down his mortgage of $350,000 with his disposable cash, instead of investing it, Don would forego over half a million dollars in potential earnings to save the equivalent of 10 years worth of interest payments. At his eight percent interest rate and assuming his mortgage is fairly new, Don could hope to save a maximum of $260,000 in interest payments. In other words Don would lose over a quarter of a million dollars by paying down his mortgage with his cash. So it was a logical and easy choice for Don to invest the funds rather than pay down the mortgage.

Since Don decided to "keep" his mortgage, he could take a tax deduction for mortgage interest, thereby reducing his income taxes. With the money that he saved on his income taxes, he was able to afford other investments, including maintaining the necessary insurance to protect his family. This further increased the benefit of his investment decision compared to paying down his mortgage.

There are also ways to restructure your mortgage that can save you money. For example, people who have sufficient disposable income can refinance with a 15-year mortgage amortization period. This results in moderately larger payments for 15 years, instead of smaller payments for 30 years, and greatly reduces the amount of interest paid over the life of the loan. This also offers the appeal of a slightly lower interest rate that saves interest in the long term, and brings closer the day of being free of the debt completely.

While accelerating your mortgage loan payments may seem like a good strategy, it should be done with great caution. Ask yourself: "If

I am laid off or disabled, or my spouse is, can I still make those large payments? Can I pay the property taxes, insurance and other housing costs?"  If the answer is "no," you may want to rethink the risk of a higher mortgage payment.  It might be better to take those extra amounts paid on your mortgage and apply them like Don did to a good mutual fund, or money market account, so that money will be available should you need it.

| $100,000 30 Year Mortgage At 7% Interest | | | |
|---|---|---|---|
| | Regular Monthly | Bi-Weekly | Monthly plus 10% |
| Payment | $665.30 | $332.64 | $731.83 |
| No. of Pay'ts | 360 | 780 | 360 |
| Total Int. Paid | $139,509 | $105,369 | $100,605 |

Another relatively painless and safe strategy is a "bi-weekly" mortgage.  With this concept you make a payment every two weeks instead of just once a month.  Each payment is about half of the amount you would otherwise pay once a month, but in the long run, you save thousands of dollars in interest over the life of the loan.  Why?  A small portion of the mid-month payment goes toward principal.  When you make a second payment later that month, you are paying against a smaller principal so the interest is then a lesser amount for the next two weeks, and so on.

In addition to the fact that you are paying down principal sooner and being charged less interest, you also are making two extra payments per year (26 instead of 24 for a twice monthly payment). Adding two more payments in a calendar year further reduces the amount of loan principal that the interest is charged against, which even further reduces your interest expense overall.

You can see from the chart above that a bi-weekly mortgage or even just increasing your monthly payment by 10% above the standard repayment amount can result in huge savings overall - between $35,000 and $40,000. Imagine taking your savings from one of these accelerated strategies, investing and seeing a return upon retirement of $100,000 or more. It is not only possible but easily achieved!

If you choose one of these accelerated payment options, but your lender wants to charge you an extra fee for the privilege of restructuring the mortgage, you can actually achieve the same net effect by paying a bit more on your monthly payment. Most loans will allow you to pay more toward the principal monthly but when sending in your payments be sure to indicate that this is your intention. Since loan agreements vary between institutions, it is important to check beforehand that prepaying your mortgage will not incur penalties or additional charges by the lender.

*Unloading Private Mortgage Insurance (PMI)*

If you took out a mortgage for more than 80% of the purchase price of your home, your lender probably insisted that you also pay for private mortgage insurance (PMI) to protect the lender in case you default. After several years of payments on that mortgage, however, you will pay down the mortgage to the point where the PMI is no longer required. At that time, you can call your lender and ask how to cancel the PMI.

Even if you haven't paid the mortgage down below 80% of the purchase price, the value of your home will almost certainly increase. Many lenders will allow you to cancel PMI if your loan amount is below 80% of the current market value of your home, regardless of the original purchase price. To support this, you will need to get an appraisal done by a local real estate firm or by an appraiser your lender approves, in order to establish its new value.

*Cozying Up to Your Uncle*

The federal government sometimes does nice things for us. One of those is allowing an employer to setup plans for pre-tax payroll deductions of medical insurance premiums, childcare expenses or out-of-pocket medical costs. This means you don't have to pay taxes on these amounts; they are deducted from your gross pay and do not count as taxable income. This reduces the amount of tax you owe, in effect giving you a discount equal to the amount of tax you would have paid on that income. If you don't itemize or if your out-of-pocket medical expenses and premiums don't exceed 7.5% of your income, you normally can't take the deduction on your tax return. Using pre-tax payroll deductions effectively gives you back this benefit!

As for childcare expenses, whether a pre-tax deduction (offered under a "cafeteria plan" and explained more fully in the next chapter) makes sense for you depends on your income level and how much these expenses are anticipated to be. Remember, if you take the childcare credit on your tax return, the allowable amount may be subtracted directly from the tax you owe. If, however, you use a pre-tax deduction pursuant to a cafeteria plan, the reduction in taxable income is limited to a maximum of $5,000 per year. Whether you pay less overall tax via a cafeteria plan or by taking the childcare tax credit depends on several factors. The best way to figure out which saves you the most money is to make yourself a cup of tea, clear off your work space, pull out last year's tax return and calculate it both ways.

# Orderly Affairs

# *Why Insurance Should Be Part of Your Financial Plan*

*"The best kind of life insurance to own is the kind that is in force when you die."*

> \- John C. Daniel,
> from "MDRT Inspirations"

It's easy to tell someone: "If life hands you lemons, make lemonade." Sometimes, however, a life crisis happens to you that is so serious that no saying will help you make the best of it. If you become disabled as the result of a car crash, for example, it can ruin you financially and leave you without the basic means to keep your home, provide for your family, or obtain the kind of care you need. That is why insurance should be a cornerstone to your financial plan -- life insurance, disability insurance and long-term care insurance.

*Life Insurance*

Barry was a man in excellent physical condition. He loved to bicycle and rode about 4,000 miles a year with his wife. He seemed in perfect health, maintained low weight and body fat levels for his age and he ate a very healthy diet.

In his early 50s, he purchased $250,000 of "term" life insurance (the type of policy that does not build up any cash value), which cost him $1,500 a year. When Barry turned 55, he and his wife started planning for retirement and wanted to cut their expenses, so they decided to eliminate the life insurance. They told their financial advisor about their intention and the advisor persuaded them to keep at least $150,000 in coverage.

Seven months later, Barry went biking in the mountains at high altitude. Due to excessive strain on his body, he suffered a heart attack and died. When his widow received the income tax-free proceeds of the death-benefit check, she was overwhelmed at the thought that she had previously agreed to terminate the entire policy. She was extremely grateful that the couple's financial advisor had persisted in getting them to hold on to at least a portion of the original policy.

Aside from the obvious goal of providing for your loved ones after your death, life insurance has other purposes. If you have substantial assets that are likely to be heavily taxed as part of your estate, life insurance can replace the money paid out in taxes or even reduce the total taxes, when arranged properly.

Life insurance is also a sort of "hidden asset" that can be tapped in certain cases. An older person who needs cash for living expenses might consider selling a life insurance policy currently in force on him to a buyer willing to make the ongoing premium payments as long as the insured survives. This strategy gives the original policyholder immediate cash. The buyer then continues the premium payments on the policy until the original insured dies, at which time the death benefit is paid to the second owner of the policy.

Life insurance companies are constantly creating new products to meet the needs of the marketplace. You should be aware of some of these important variations now available:

- Variable life insurance policy - these products offer investment choices, tax-deferred accumulation and tax-preferred access to the cash values.

- Life insurance with long-term care riders - this type of policy allows the insured to receive proceeds from the policy during their lifetime to meet the needs of paying for long-term care. The benefit is based on a percentage of the death benefit when accessed.

- Survivorship policies - these are commonly used to cover more than one individual. The death benefit normally pays to the named beneficiary at the death of the last surviving insured.

- Critical care policies - named, specific, life-threatening events will trigger the payment of a defined amount of money to the insured to pay for expenses the insured deems necessary for their care and well-being. It is meant to cover situations where a catastrophic (terminal) illness occurs.

Whole life insurance, universal life insurance and term insurance are all types of life insurance products commonly purchased from insurance companies. Be sure to work with your advisor to clearly understand the death benefit(s) provided, cash values created over time and the tax consequences of each choice (if any).

Since policies vary, each policy needs to be reviewed to find the best solution for the insured. Several different quotations from different companies should be gathered before making a decision on which is the best choice for the insured. Remember to discuss your insurance needs in the context of your overall financial goals and strategies. Your advisor should be aware in the event that you may want to pursue the option of selling the policy to a third party buyer. Under other policies available, the owner of life insurance may surrender the policy in later years for its cash value and receive portions of the money back tax-free. This is usually an option one would pursue only to provide cash at a critical time.

*Disability Insurance*

Eric, a shipping-company executive, made about $5,000 a month; his wife, Susana, was a paralegal making about $3,000 a month. The couple counted on Susana's income to pay for their home mortgage.

They did not have disability insurance for Susana, while Eric was covered through his employer. This situation put them at substantial risk because if Susana became disabled, for any reason, they would no longer be able to pay their mortgage and could lose their house.

Eric was reluctant to purchase disability coverage on Susana because the annual cost was about $1,600. He finally moved forward and paid the first installment of $400 for three months of coverage. When the next payment came due, he paid that too but he had,by then, decided to drop the coverage at the end of six months.

Three weeks later, Susana, who was only 43 at the time, was permanently disabled in a car accident. Because the couple had disability insurance, Susana was able to receive more than $1,800 per month for the rest of her working years, until she turned 65. This amount represented 60% of her former income and was paid out as a tax-free benefit. The total amount she received was ultimately $475,200, with no further premiums required after she became disabled. She was also eligible to receive disability benefits from Social Security for herself and her young son.

As a result of the disability insurance Eric had taken out for Susana, the couple could not only hold onto their home, but they also had enough money to invest in additional real estate in the years that followed. Now that Eric is retired, the couple can live quite comfortably on the combined income from his retirement benefits, their combined Social Security, real estate investment income and her disability insurance income.

*Long-Term Care Insurance*

In past generations, when family members became too ill or infirm to take care of themselves, the rest of the family would pitch in as best they could to care for them. This burden often fell on a stay-at-home spouse or unmarried children to provide the care required.

Today, in a society that has become increasingly mobile and where "nuclear" families are spread over increasingly greater distances, it becomes very difficult to count on this kind of care. In the United States, where both husband and wife are often working full time and the children are in school all day, it can be next to impossible to take care of a stay-at-home senior who needs around-the-clock 24-hour a day care.

The bottom line is that we can no longer expect our children or extended families to turn their lives upside down to take care of us when we can no longer take care of ourselves. Note that this is a situation that can happen to anyone, at any age. Ill health and disability are not confined to the elderly; an accident or catastrophic illness can radically change the life of even the young. Of all people in nursing homes in 1998, 40% were under the age of 65!

It may come as a shock to many people that, when it comes to providing this kind of long-term care, government programs are woefully lacking. More and more people today are securing private long-term care insurance to make sure they can live at home with fully paid care services or receive paid for care in a facility of their own choosing should the need arise.

SAM

At 70, Sam started showing signs of Alzheimer's disease. His wife, Diane, initially tried to take care of Sam full time. Their two children, who lived nearby, also provided assistance. Eventually, though, Sam needed full-time supervision and the family arranged for home health workers to assist them, at $18 an hour. After a year, even this was not sufficient to care for Sam, and he was placed in a nursing home that was not covered by Medicare. Overall, the family spent more than $50,000 per year out of their own limited budget on Sam's care.

If Sam had long-term care insurance coverage, the family would not have had to drain their savings making sure that their loved one was cared for adequately. While long-term care policies may seem expensive when purchased, in the longer term they can help a family preserve their hard-won assets and avoid a financial disaster. They can also serve to protect the individual covered from being placed in facilities provided by the government, which may be less than ideal.

What long-term care policies do, above all else, is provide choices that otherwise wouldn't be available, during a difficult and stressful time in people's lives. It is now more important than ever to ensure that, when we suffer a health setback, we can receive adequate care and have our expenses paid for by properly designed long-term care policies that meet our needs.

*Association Plans, Medical Savings Accounts, Cafeteria Plans*

When you work for someone else, more than likely you have little choice about the kind of insurance coverage you get. There may, however, be other avenues for you to secure the kinds of insurance that really fit your needs.

Do you belong to a professional association? A union? Do you work for the government? Even if you have retired, you may belong to a retiree' group or qualify to be a member of an "alumni" association. If so, you may have an "association plan" available to you that can fill some of the gaps in your present insurance coverage.

*Group Insurance vs. Association Plans*

Group insurance is a contract with the group itself as the insured, rather than with the individuals in the group. Coverage is evidenced by "certificates of coverage" rather than individual policies. Generally this coverage is less expensive, however, the insurance provider can cancel its contract with the group (which it has the right to do). The individuals in the group could lose their coverage or experience significantly higher costs for individual policies with reduced benefits.

Association plans, on the other hand, are contracts with individual members of an association. These contracts are not cancelable as long as the premiums continue to be paid. Furthermore, the individual may leave the association and still continue the coverage.

Qualifying for coverage is usually less restrictive than in the open market, and individuals can tailor benefits to their specific needs and budget. Members' extended family, by blood or marriage, the old or the young, may also be able to obtain coverage through the member's association plan. Premiums are not subject to annual adjustment, although they may be increased for the entire class of insureds. The cost of coverage may be lower for members in the association, and some policies even provide additional benefits not normally provided in individual policies. For example, a long-term care policy might include an accidental-death benefit, ambulance service and prescription drug benefits for nursing home stays.

There are some drawbacks. Members do not automatically qualify for coverage and there may be more restrictions or reduced overall benefits on these policies than if coverage were provided outside such a group.

*Getting the Most out of Your Paycheck*

You have already discovered that only a portion of medical expenses may be deductible on your tax return, or may not be deductible at all based on certain medical thresholds under the itemized deduction categories (e.g. only the amount that exceeds 7.5% of your adjusted gross income is deductible).

You need to ask yourself: are you having ongoing medical procedures done that are a regular out-of-pocket expense? Does a close family member need long-term care requiring services not covered by any insurance? The way to cover these expenses may rest with a one of the alternative plans described below.

The equivalent of a tax deduction for medical expenses that otherwise might not be available can sometimes be obtained through a Medical Savings Account (MSA), a Medical Reimbursement Plan or a Cafeteria Plan. Simply put, these plans allow you to set aside funds with pre-tax dollars. Upon your instructions, your employer deducts a set amount from each paycheck and places it in a separate account for your benefit. The purpose of these plans is to provide for your non-covered medical, childcare and other expenses. You then pay your medical expenses personally and draw reimbursement from the account on a pre-tax basis.

*Medical Savings Accounts*

The MSA is available to self-employed individuals (and their spouses), and members of employer groups of 50 or fewer, when they carry a high-deductible health plan. It is established with pre-tax dollars to reimburse medical expenses such as deductibles and co-payments. An MSA provides several benefits:

- The money can be used tax-free for all qualified medical expenses;

- Any balance you do not use can be rolled over from year to year tax free;

- If you earn interest on the money in the account it is also tax free;

Some of the expenses that MSAs may be used for are:

- Dental
- Acupuncture
- Psychological services
- Chiropractic
- Vision
- Long-term care insurance
- Continuation coverage such as COBRA
- Health plan premiums paid while you receive unemployment compensation.

Is this sounding too good to be true? There is a ceiling on how much you can contribute to an MSA. For an individual, it is 65% of the annual medical plan deductible; for families, it is 75% of the annual deductible. There may be other limitations, so be sure to check with your advisor.

*Medical Reimbursement Plans*

An employer may set up a Medical Reimbursement Plan to reimburse employees for medical expenses not covered by their regular medical insurance, such as dental expenses and costs above policy limits. The employee generally receives payments tax-free. The employer makes payments into the account on a tax-deductible basis.

*Cafeteria Plans*

Also called "Flexible Benefit Plans" or "125 Plans", Cafeteria Plans are employee-funded plans that allow individuals to pay for childcare costs and non-covered medical expenses with pre-tax dollars. The table that follows lists examples of medical-related expenses allowed under Cafeteria Plans.

As of 2002, the limit on annual contributions to this type of plan is $5,000 per family. There is one overriding limitation of Cafeteria Plans: the employee forfeits any funds remaining in the plan at the end of the benefit year. It is very important, then, not to overestimate the amount needed for out-of-pocket expenses.

# Examples of Expenses Eligible for Reimbursement as Part of a Cafeteria Plan

Acupuncture
Alcoholism treatment
Ambulance hire
Artificial limbs
Artificial teeth
Birth control pills
Braces
Braille - books and magazines
Car controls for handicapped
Care for mentally handicapped child
Childcare expenses
Chiropractors
Christian Science practitioners' fees
Co-insurance amounts you pay
Contact lenses (includes solution)
Cosmetic surgery (non-elective)
Cost of operations and related treatments
Crutches
Daycare expenses for eligible dependents
   as necessary due to employment
Deductible medical coverage amounts
   you pay
Dental fees
Dentures
Diagnostic fees
Drug and medical supplies
Electrolysis (non-elective)
Eyeglasses (including examination fee)
Fees of practical nurse
Fees for healing services
Handicapped persons' special schools
Health insurance (including Medicare
Part B payments, but Part A coverage
is not deductible unless person is 65
or over and is not entitled to Social
Security benefits)
Hearing devices and batteries
Home improvements motivated by
   medical considerations
Hospital bills
Hospitalization insurance
Hypnosis for treatment of an illness
Insulin
Laboratory fees
Laetrile by prescription

Membership fees in association with
   furnishing medical services,
   hospitalization and clinical care
Nurses' fees (including nurses/ board and
   Social Security tax where paid by
   taxpayer)
Obstetrical expenses
Operations
Orthopedic shoes
Oxygen
Physician fees
Physician-prescribed swimming pool or
   spa equipment cost and maintenance
Physician-prescribed weight loss or
   smoking cessation programs
Psychiatric care
Psychologist fees
Retarded persons' cost for special home/
   homecare
Routine physicals and other diagnostic
   Services or treatments
Seeing eye dog and its upkeep
Smoking cessation program (if prescribed
by a physician)
Special diets (if prescribed by a physician)
Special education for the blind
Special plumbing for the handicapped
Sterilization fees
Surgical fees
Telephone, special design for deaf
Television audio display equipment for deaf
Therapeutic care for drug and alcohol addition
Therapy treatment
Transportation expenses primarily in the
rendering of medical services, i.e., railroad
fare to hospital or to recuperation home,
cab fare in obstetrical cases
Tuition at special school for handicapped
Tuition fee (part) if college or private school
furnishes breakdown of medical charges
Vitamins by prescription
Weight loss program if prescribed by a doctor
Wheelchair
Wigs (non-elective)
X-rays

Provided by Nicholas & Hicks Inc., Legal and Pension Consultants

# *Home, Sweet Home*

*"It is a comfortable feeling to know that you stand on your own ground.  Land is about the only thing that can't fly away."*
- "The Last Chronicle of Barset",
by Anthony Trollope

It is the dream of virtually every American family to own their own home. Often, however, no matter how much or how long they save, families find that the home that they want is just out of reach. Sometimes a little creativity and compromise can help you achieve your dream.

MIKE

In 1984, Mike and his wife purchased a half-acre of land in a San Francisco suburb for $75,000, a bargain at the time. However, the property did not just fall into their laps. Mike had looked for property in an area where the population was increasing, since this made it more likely the property would appreciate in value. He was patient in his search for the right parcel, looking for two and a half years before finding the right combination of qualities.

Upon closing, they paid $37,500 in cash and borrowed the rest of the money. The lot had a rustic but habitable 1,000 square foot cabin on it, which Mike and his family chose to fix up and live in for about two years.

During the two years the family lived in the cabin, they paid a very low monthly mortgage amount and were able to get ahead financially. After two years, they decided to build their dream home and took out a loan to construct a beautiful 3,000-square-foot house, moving into it in 1986. The property was now appraised at $350,000.

*An Opportunity to Do Some Good*

When the new house was built, the family decided to look for a way to donate the existing cabin to an organization that could use it to benefit a family in need. The worthwhile charity Habitat for Humanity was contacted and they arranged for removal of the structure. Not only did this ultimately help another family but it also allowed Mike and his wife to take a charitable deduction of $75,000 against taxable income over a three-year period (based upon an MIA appraisal of the structure). This allowed for the recovery of about half the original purchase price of the property as a tax benefit.

The initial purchase price, plus construction of a new home, made for a total investment in the property of $240,000. Seventeen years later, the property was worth about $750,000, a 20-fold increase over the original cash investment.

Mike and his family achieved these very impressive results by being patient, waiting for the right opportunity to come along, and being willing to do some or all of the improvements needed themselves in order to add value to the property. Here is a summary list of steps they took that resulted in the realization of their dream home, starting with very little equity:

- Mike and his wife built up their property's value using sweat equity, building part of the house themselves, thus minimizing their debt.

- They took advantage of a large charitable tax deduction, using the money saved from their taxes to wipe out indebtedness from purchase of the property.

- They increased the value of the property by building a much nicer home, in keeping with other homes in the neighborhood.

- They increased their net worth by investing in real estate (their home).

- They gave back to the community by donating the cabin. This, in turn, helped someone else become a homeowner.

HABITAT FOR HUMANITY

This organization, in which former President Jimmy Carter is very active, was founded in 1976 by Millard and Linda Fuller as a nonprofit ecumenical Christian housing ministry. It welcomes people of all faiths to its work. Its purpose is to "build simple, decent, affordable houses in partnership with those in need of adequate shelter." The organization has been involved in projects across the United States and around the world.

Through volunteer labor and donations of money and materials, Habitat builds and rehabilitates simple, decent houses with the help of the prospective homeowner families. Habitat houses are sold to those families at no profit, financed with affordable, no-interest loans. The homeowners' monthly mortgage payments are used to build still more Habitat homes. In addition to a down payment and the monthly mortgage payments, homeowners invest hundreds of hours of their own labor -- sweat equity -- into building their Habitat house and the houses of others like them.

Worldwide, the cost of the houses varies from as little as $800 in developing countries to an average of $46,600 in the United States.

To contact Habitat for Humanity, call the Habitat help line at (800) 422-4828, extension 2551 or 2552, or go online to www.habitat.org.

# Orderly Affairs

# *Start Retiring Now*

*"Lose this day loitering-'twill be the same story,*
*To-morrow and the next more dilatory;*
*Each indecision brings its own delays,*
*And days are lost lamenting o'er lost days."*
                           - from Faust by
                           Johanne Wolfgang von Goethe

## JANICE

Janice went to work for the gas company at age 18, and over the next 22 years was able to amass $650,000 in retirement benefits. At age 42 she retired, moved her money to an IRA account where it continued to grow and was valued a few years later at over $1.1 million. At that point in time, her financial advisor and her attorney recommended that she consider a special "72T" election for distribution of funds from the IRA account without penalty. The idea was for her to withdraw funds from her retirement account during her late 40s and early 50s, ensuring an adequate cash flow so that she would be able to go back to school and start a new business of her own.

By following this advice, Janice was able to realize her dream of completely changing her career by, in effect, retiring early. It also provided sufficient income to pay off her house in approximately five years, fund her new business, travel, and spend time with family and friends.

Most people who work for a living daydream about what they will do when they retire - and many of us wouldn't mind retiring tomorrow if we could! No matter how young you are, it makes sense to start planning for retirement now. Saving for retirement can reduce your current income taxes and - if you work for a company that matches your contributions to a 401(k) plan - you can even reap the benefit of money that didn't come out of your own pocket. If you are self-employed, you will most likely use an IRA or Keogh plan. If you work for a company that has no 401(k), then an IRA is also probably what you will use.

Here's how it works. With most IRAs and 401(k)s (except for Roth IRAs), money contributed to these accounts is "pre-tax", that is, you don't pay income tax on it until you start withdrawing it for your retirement. This not only defers taxes you would have had to pay on the contributions, it can also result in less actual tax paid, if you are taxed at a lower marginal tax rate at the time you make your withdrawals in retirement. If you plan carefully, this will result in the IRS actually granting you a legal tax avoidance strategy.

Here are the different types of preferred retirement plans allowed by law.

*Traditional IRA (Individual Retirement Account)*

An IRA is a trust or custodial account established by an individual with a bank or qualified firm that acts as a trustee or custodian of investments. The investments are contributed by the individual or purchased with funds contributed by the individual.

There are many different varieties or versions of the IRA concept. For example: an individual retirement annuity is a contract issued by an insurance company; the individual pays premiums instead of contributions. A group IRA is a plan sponsored by an employer or labor union. With the advent of simplified employee pensions (SEP's) and simple IRAs, group IRAs are now rarely used.

Contribution limits to IRAs are based upon earned income, as well as adjusted gross income (AGI). As of January 1, 2002, contribution limits are $3,000 per year. That limit will rise each year until it reaches $5,000 per year in 2008. As of 2002, the combined total maximum contribution for both spouses is $6,000 (the tax deduction is computed separately for each spouse).

IRAs associated with employer-sponsored SEPs and Simple IRAs are essentially traditional IRAs with special rules. The only real distinction between a SEP-IRA and a traditional IRA is the annual contribution limit. The SEP-IRA is treated like a qualified profit-sharing plan in which the employer may contribute up to 15% of a worker's compensation (with a limit of $160,000 on compensation used for this calculation), or $30,000 (whichever is less).

*Roth IRA*

Created in 1997, the Roth IRA can be important for people who do not qualify for the traditional IRA deduction. Roth IRAs allow individuals to make after-tax contributions, have earnings on their contributions accumulate free of income tax, and receive tax-free distributions. As of January 1, 2002, the annual contribution for a Roth IRA is $3,000 of earned income for each spouse. The $3,000 limit is reduced by the amount of the individual's contributions to a traditional IRA in that year. The allowable Roth IRA annual contribution limits phase out for those individuals making $95,000 to $110,000 per year and couples making $150,000 to $160,000.

*Keogh Plans*

This is a special investment plan for self-employed individuals. Contribution limits are more liberal than for IRAs (as of 2002, this is $30,000) allowing a self-employed person to contribute considerably more to a tax deductible retirement savings account than a traditional IRA.

*401(k) Plans*

401(k) retirement savings plans are offered by many employers and allow up to $30,000 (as of 2002) per year per employee to be contributed. Funds may be contributed solely by the employee or by both the employee and employer using a variety of matching contribution arrangements. Employer contributions can be in the form of cash or stock (including options). The limits allowed under 401(k) contribution rules will gradually increase under new tax laws.

The vast array of retirement savings plans available can leave individuals feeling confused about what should be their best strategy to achieve financial independence at retirement. The strategy for retirement planning can best be illustrated by an acquaintance of ours.

JIM

Jim worked from the time he was 20 years old until he retired at age 62. During those years, he set aside money in his 401(k) plan each year at the maximum amount allowed. At retirement, Jim had approximately $750,000 in his account. At that time, he decided to roll it over to an IRA using a trustee-to-trustee transfer. Having it in an IRA account, he was then able take withdrawals from it as he wished. This means that he was able to retire, receive Social Security, have an income from his other investments plus his IRA account, and live on those funds for the rest of his life. He also maintained control of how much income he took annually from his IRA in order to determine how much tax he wished to pay each year.

The key to any type of tax-deferred retirement savings plan is to start as soon as possible. For example, assuming that around $10,000 per year goes into your retirement plan, and assuming that you receive a 10% annual return on investment, you will have about $600,000 in your plan in 20 years. At the end of 25 years, you would have almost $1 million in the account - a net increase of roughly $400,000 in the last five years. Obviously, the sooner you start, the better!

# Features of Popular Retirement Plans*

| Plan type | Funded by | Contributions are tax-deductible | Maximum annual contribution |
|---|---|---|---|
| Defined benefit plan | The employer who offers the plan | Yes, to the contributing employer | Contributions must fit targeted benefits which can't exceed $200,000 or 100% of includable compensation-cost of living increases after 2002 |
| Traditional IRA | Individuals | Yes, unless the participant is covered by another plan and income exceeds certain levels | Lesser of $3,000 ($3,500 if 50 or older) plus $3,000 for non-working spouse (less contrib. to all other IRAs) or 100% of the individual's compensation for the year |
| Roth IRA | Individuals | No, but qualified distributions are income-tax free | Lesser of $3,000 ($3,500 if 50 or older) less contributions to all other IRAs) or 100% of the individual's compensation for the year |
| SEP-IRA | The employer who offers the plan | Yes, to contributing employer | Lesser of $30,000 or 15% of includable compensation (13.043% or $40,000 of earned income for self-employed) (COL increases after 2002) |
| Money Purchase | The employer who offers the plan | Yes, to the contributing employer | Lesser of $35,000 or 25% of includable compensation (COL increases after 2002) |
| Profit-Sharing Plan | The employer who offers the plan | Yes, to the contributing employer | Lesser of $35,000 or 25% of includable compensation; 15% overall limit (cost of living increases after 2002) |
| Simple Plan | Employees of the company offering | Yes, to the contributing employee the plan | Generally, employee pre-tax salary deferral contributions of up to $7,000 in 2002 (increasing $1,000 each year to $10,000 in 2005 (COL increases aterwards. |
| 401(k) Plan | Employees; Employers can fund | Yes, to the contributing employee and employer | $11,000 (increasing to $15,000 in 2006- COL increases afterwards) or 25% of includable compensation |
| 403(b) Custodial Account | Employees of educational, char-itable, scientific or religious organ-izations | Yes, to the contributing employee | Lesser of $8,500 or 33% of salary |

*Rules and regulations of retirement plans are constantly changing. Consult your financial advisor.

# Orderly Affairs

# Saving for Your Children's College Education

*"Do you know the best time to plant an oak tree? Forty years ago. Do you know the next best time? Today."*
                                        - Larry J. Buessing

College funding has been an objective of families for over 100 years. A new college savings plan has become available over the last few years that is highly "tax preferred" but still relatively unknown to the general public.

When §529 of the tax code was enacted in 1996, it gave states the power to sponsor higher education savings plans called Qualified State Tuition Programs (QSTPs). These QSTPs have several features and benefits, including federal and state tax deferral, no income limits, and substantial contribution maximums. Perhaps just as significant are the unique and generous gift and estate tax features that accompany QSTPs, including the ability to remove assets from the taxable estate while retaining control over their use.

States have been slow to roll these plans out, however Georgia and South Dakota still have no plans. Most states have limited marketing resources to get the word out to the general public; and, as a result, the plan remains relatively unknown. In addition, financial advisors have not been involved in setting up these plans, but instead the states have tended to use direct sales via an 800 number, further limiting the reach of the program.

To get a better understanding of why someone would use a 529 plan, let's explore some of its key advantages, drawbacks, and strategies.

*Advantages*

- Tax-free growth without limitation on the amount held within the plan is available at the federal and, in most cases, state level in 529 plans. When the funds are used for qualified higher-education expenses, the distributions are withdrawn free of federal tax.

• Control of disbursements remains with the account owner in 529 plans, despite the fact that the creation of the account is a completed gift and removes the assets from the taxable estate of the account owner. This is a significant advantage when compared to an UGMA/UTMA (Uniform Gift to Minors Act/Uniform Trust for Minors Act) account, which typically transfers control to the beneficiary upon 18 years of age.

# Estate Planning Benefits Illustration
## College Savings Plan Estate Tax Benefit

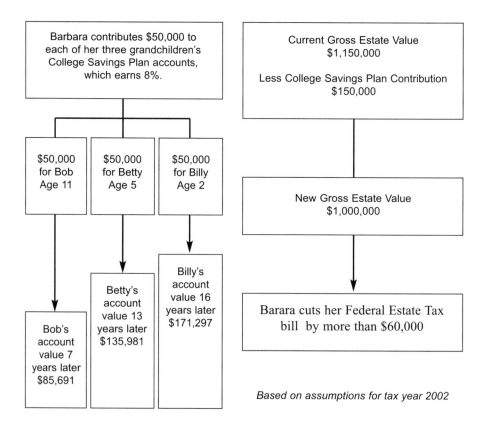

*Based on assumptions for tax year 2002*

- Ability to change the beneficiary is offered by 529 programs. Should the beneficiary not need the 529 funds, or if there are excess funds after paying for college and graduate school, the account's beneficiary can be changed to a wide range of relatives of the original beneficiary. With the signing of the 2001 Tax Relief Act, beneficiary changes have now been extended to include cousins of the original beneficiary.

- Estate planning needs can also be met while saving for college using 529 plans. Unlike other estate planning vehicles, significant assets can be moved out of the taxable estate of the donor, while the donor retains control of the disbursement of the funds. Through a simple election, a donor can contribute up to $50,000 in one year for each beneficiary ($100,000 if married) without gift tax consequences (see diagram below). Any excess contributions made during this period will incur gift taxes, which are credited against a participant's lifetime gift exclusion (currently $1,000,000). These contributions are also subject to an "add back" rule in the event of the donor's death within five years.

- High maximum contribution limits are offered by several states' 529 programs (each state sets its own maximum contribution.) The maximum contribution will, in the future, be adjusted upward with college tuition inflation (see diagram below). The highest limit is currently more than $245,000, calculated as the cost of five years of undergraduate and two years of graduate education at the institutions with the highest cost of attendance per year in that state.

There are broad definitions of eligible expenses and institutions. Eligible expenses include tuition, room and board, and supplies. Eligible institutions are all those eligible to participate in U.S. Department of Education student aid programs (more than 8,000 institutions), which includes colleges, universities, community colleges and certain technical schools.

# The Rising Cost of College
## The Cost of a Four-Year Education
### (Tuition, Fees, Room & Board)

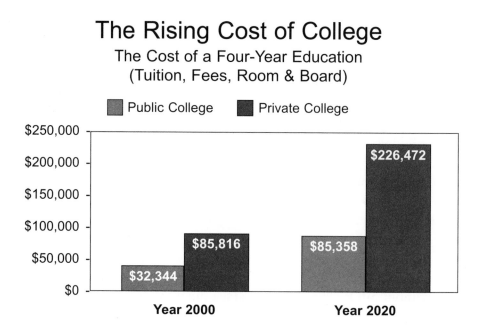

- Most 529 savings plans allow minimum initial contributions of just $250 to establish an account. No initial contribution is required for payroll deduction and ACH (Automated Clearing House) participation in many states. Very low (e.g., $10) commitments are available for such periodic funding methods.

- Professional money management is offered by most 529 programs. Though some states use their own investment personnel to manage the assets in their 529 plans, most states contract with professional investment companies to manage the funds and look after record keeping.

- Penalty-free withdrawals are available in the event of the death or disability of a beneficiary, or the receipt of a scholarship by the beneficiary. All penalty-free withdrawals are still subject to taxation on the gains at ordinary income rates for the beneficiary.

*Drawbacks*

- The primary restriction on 529 plans is that program assets must be used for higher education expenses to avoid penalties. Should the account owner make a non-qualified withdrawal, a penalty of 10% must be assessed against the gains on the original contribution (there is a pro-rata split between contributions and gains for each withdrawal). The gains, on non-qualified withdrawals, will also be taxed as income to the account owner at their current marginal income tax rate.

UGMA/UTMA transfers to 529 plans have proven to be popular. Beneficiaries do not gain control of the assets at the age of majority under a 529 program, as they do under UGMA/UTMA. However, the original UGMA/UTMA beneficiary becomes "locked in" and cannot be changed and only the named beneficiary can utilize the funds in the accounts.

Existing 529 plan-to-plan transfers will increase as more plans are launched. With approximately $10 billion already in 529 savings products, a significant amount of 529 assets are expected to be shifted to the newer, more flexible multiple investment option programs. In particular, participants will make transfer decisions based on investment performance and fund management.
It has become quite clear that with the costs of both public and

private universities skyrocketing, there is a serious need for an efficient funding vehicle. The 529 plans give us the best opportunity yet to be able to send our children to the college of their choice.

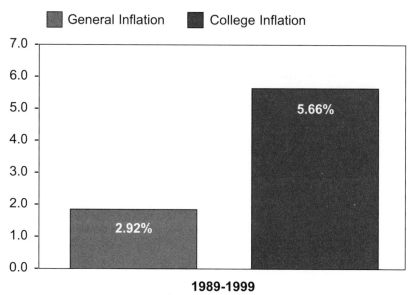

During the 1990s, college costs increased at twice the rate of annualized inflation.

1989-1999

*Source: BLS, Independent College 500 (TM) Index*

## BARBARA AND MARK

Barbara and Mark set up a series of irrevocable "educational trusts" to pay for the college educations of three of their six grandchildren.

The educational trusts were designed to invest money for the benefit of the grandchildren without having the trust income subject to income tax until each grandchild reached the age of 21. At that point, a special tax would be assessed to "catch up" on any income or capital gains that had accrued on the investments.

Their financial advisor informed them that under the new 2001 Tax Relief Act, a 529 plan could be utilized by the client in lieu of irrevocable trusts.  Parents can also set up 529 plans for their children.

To summarize, the 529 Program provides:

- Tax-deferred growth of the investment.

- Tax-free distribution of the principal and income to the beneficiary, if the distribution is used for a qualified educational purpose.

- The ability of the grandparents/parents in an emergency to withdraw the funds from the 529 Program for their own use (subject to tax on any gain and penalty - consult your advisor).

- The ability to change beneficiaries.

- Removal of the assets in the 529 from the grandparents'/parents' taxable estate.

- The simplicity of administering a 529 plan, compared to an irrevocable trust.  For example, irrevocable trusts require trustees and annual income tax returns.  529 plans do not.

- High contribution limits that would actually cover the cost of an education, as opposed to the severe limitations of other funding vehicles.

Barbara and Mark were so impressed with how the new 529 program works that they decided to redirect funds designated for the irrevocable trusts established for their grandchildren so that the money would be put directly into a 529 program.

# Orderly Affairs

# *Annuities*

*"If one advances confidently in the direction of his dreams, and endeavors to live the life which he has imagined, he will meet with a success unexpected in common hours."*
- Henry David Thoreau

As a result of an overwhelming need for retirement planning, annuities have become extremely popular.

An annuity is a contract sold by a life insurance company, which guarantees either a fixed or variable payment at some future time, such as retirement. Some of the benefits that annuities offer as retirement planning vehicles are:

- Tax Deferral - Funds that are placed in an annuity grow on a tax-deferred basis (and are not subject to current income taxes). This can have a significant impact on the amount that accumulates over time.

  As an example, see the accompanying charts. The first graphically illustrates that the amount of time for your money to double in value increases by 50% (from 8 to 12 years) assuming a 33% tax rate versus a tax deferred option. After 24 years, the amount of money attained is doubled by the power of tax deferred growth.

  In the second chart, the growth attained by starting with a lowly penny and doubling it's value every day is shown for the case of taxable (at two different tax brackets) and tax deferred growth. The amounts accumulated after 31 days show a remarkable disparity; from just over $14,000 at the higher tax bracket to over ten million dollars if growth is allowed to accumulate tax deferred!

- Guaranteed Principal as a Death Benefit - This is a key benefit for those who are concerned about leaving funds to a beneficiary. This benefit allows the contract owner to participate in the stock

# The Power of Tax-Deferral

By using the Rule of 72, you are able to approximate the number of years it takes to double your investment at a given rate of return. As you can see below, tax deferral can help you accumulate money faster AND potentially provide more spendable income after taxes.

**The Rule of 72:**   $\dfrac{72}{\text{Growth rate}}$   **= Estimated number of years needed to double your investment**

## Accumulate More Money in Less Time...

| **Taxable Illustration** | **Tax-Deferred Illustration** |
|---|---|
| $100,000 starting investment | $100,000 starting investment |
| 9% rate of return | 9% rate of return |
| 33% tax rate | 0% tax rate |
| 33% tax rate on 9% = 6% net | 0% tax rate on 9% = 9% net |

| | | |
|---|---|---|
| $\dfrac{72}{6\%}$ = 12 years | | $\dfrac{72}{9\%}$ = 8 years |

| | | | | |
|---|---|---|---|---|
| $100,000 | start | | $100,000 | start |
| $200,000 | 12 years | | $200,000 | 8 years |
| $400,000 | 24 years | | $400,000 | 16 years |
| $800,000 | 36 years | | $800,000 | 24 years |

## ...and Have More Spendable Retirement Income

| | |
|---|---|
| after 24 years: | after 24 years: |
| $400,000 | $800,000 |
| 10% income | 10% income |
| $40,000 pre-tax income | $80,000 pre-tax income |
| 28% tax rate | 28% tax rate |
| $28,800 after tax | $57,600 after tax |

This illustration is intended solely to demonstrate the comparative effect of compounding on taxable versus non-taxable investments. It does not reflect the actual return of any product or investment. Withdrawals of taxable amounts are subject to income tax, and a 10% IRS tax penalty may apply to withdrawals prior to 59½. No legal or tax advice is provided. We suggest that you contact your attorney, accountant or tax advisor for information concerning your particular circumstances.

## The Power of *Tax-Deferred* Compounding

| Day | Double With No Tax | Double With Tax @ 28% | Double With Tax @ 39.6% |
|---|---|---|---|
| 1 | $ 0.01 | $ 0.01 | $ 0.01 |
| 2 | $ 0.02 | $ 0.02 | $ 0.02 |
| 3 | $ 0.04 | $ 0.03 | $ 0.03 |
| 4 | $ 0.08 | $ 0.05 | $ 0.04 |
| 5 | $ 0.16 | $ 0.09 | $ 0.07 |
| 6 | $ 0.32 | $ 0.15 | $ 0.11 |
| 7 | $ 0.64 | $ 0.26 | $ 0.17 |
| 8 | $ 1.28 | $ 0.45 | $ 0.27 |
| 9 | $ 2.56 | $ 0.77 | $ 0.44 |
| 10 | $ 5.12 | $ 1.32 | $ 0.70 |
| 11 | $ 10.24 | $ 2.27 | $ 1.13 |
| 12 | $ 20.48 | $ 3.90 | $ 1.81 |
| 13 | $ 40.96 | $ 6.70 | $ 2.90 |
| 14 | $ 81.92 | $ 11.53 | $ 4.65 |
| 15 | $ 163.84 | $ 19.83 | $ 7.46 |
| 16 | $ 327.68 | $ 34.11 | $ 11.97 |
| 17 | $ 655.36 | $ 58.68 | $ 19.20 |
| 18 | $ 1,310.72 | $ 100.92 | $ 30.79 |
| 19 | $ 2,621.44 | $ 173.58 | $ 49.39 |
| 20 | $ 5,242.88 | $ 298.57 | $ 79.23 |
| 21 | $ 10,485.76 | $ 513.53 | $ 127.08 |
| 22 | $ 20,971.52 | $ 883.28 | $ 203.84 |
| 23 | $ 41,943.04 | $ 1,519.24 | $ 326.96 |
| 24 | $ 83,886.08 | $ 2,613.09 | $ 524.45 |
| 25 | $ 167,772.16 | $ 4,494.51 | $ 841.21 |
| 26 | $ 335,544.32 | $ 7,730.56 | $ 1,349.30 |
| 27 | $ 671,088.64 | $ 13,296.57 | $ 2,164.28 |
| 28 | $ 1,342,177.28 | $ 22,870.10 | $ 3,471.51 |
| 29 | $ 2,684,354.56 | $ 39,336.57 | $ 5,568.29 |
| 30 | $ 5,368,709.12 | $ 67.658.90 | $ 8,931.54 |
| 31 | $ 10,737,418.24 | $ 116,373.32 | $14,326.20 |

market, knowing the original investment is protected in the event that the value is less than anticipated.

- Guaranteed Lifetime Income - This is a major reason annuities are used for retirement planning. There are several income options that can be selected with each one providing a guarantee that income will last for at least the rest of the annuitant's lifetime, or longer.

- Unlimited Contribution Limits - There are no limits on the amount that can be invested in an annuity contract. This bypasses the problem that people face when other vehicles are used, such as a traditional IRA or Roth IRA.

Insurance companies that offer annuities continuously refine and improve their products for the benefit of the consumer. Some of the latest improvements include specialized options and features (known as "riders"). These riders provide life insurance and/or long-term care benefits that can be added to the contract without the necessity of underwriting or insurability questions being asked as is common with life insurance applications and policies. This means that someone who could not qualify for these benefits under regular life, disability or long-term care insurance can now have these benefits added to an annuity contract without health or other insurability complications being an issue.

Another important rider that has been developed for annuities is the Earnings Enhancement Benefit (EEB). This benefit provides an additional payout on death based on a percentage of the growth in the contract. For example, if a contract increases in value by $100,000 above the original purchase amount, the insurance company would provide a death benefit of up to as much as 50%, or $50,000, of that increased value. This rider would provide, at death, an enhancement to the policy that would cover most of the estate tax liability or income tax liability as the case may be. (If this issue applies to you, be sure to ask your tax advisor about the tax credit called "income in respect of a decedent".)

Note that you may also purchase an annuity with funds from an IRA account. This may be in the form of a deferred or immediate annuity.

Each provides different benefits based upon your needs.

If your employer provides a 401(k) plan option it may include the use of an annuity product that has, as its investment vehicle, sub-accounts with various investment options. Funds flowing into a 401(k) annuity contract are pre-tax dollars. All funds, including the growth on the annuity dollars, are taxable when taken out through a qualified distribution (generally at retirement). An exception to this rule is if funds are borrowed from the 401(k) under a five-year payback regulation. You should review this, as with any investment and borrowing strategy, with your financial advisor.

The following chart provides general guidelines only for non-qualified contracts, and does not cover all possible scenarios. Death is assumed to occur prior to the contract's maturity date. No legal or tax advice is provided. Each client's situation is unique, and should be reviewed by his or her attorney or accountant prior to electing or changing owners, annuitants or beneficiaries of a contract. We recommend beneficiary designations be reviewed on an annual basis to ensure proceeds are paid to the intended recipient(s).

*5-year rule: If a non-spouse beneficiary elects to take the death benefit as a settlement option, it must be for five years or over the lifetime of the beneficiary. The election must be made within one year of death. Spousal beneficiaries are not subject to the forced distribution five-year rule or to the requirement that they elect a settlement option based on life/life contingency.

| Owner | Annuitant | Proper Death of | Ownership of Annuities Death Claims Payments |
|---|---|---|---|
| Individual | Same individual | Individual | Death benefit is paid to the beneficiary in lump sum of settlement option under the 5-year rule.* If beneficiary is owner's surviving spouse, he or she may continue the contract. |
| Individual | Different individual | Annuitant | Owner becomes the annuitant. |
| Individual | Different joint individuals | 1 annuitant | Contract remains in force. |
| Individual | Joint | Both annuitants | If owner is alive, owner becomes the annuitant. If owner is not alive, death benefit is paid to beneficiary in lump sum or settlement option under the 5-year rule.* If beneficiary is owner's surviving spouse, he or she may continue the contract. |
| Individual | Joint | Owner | Death benefit paid to the beneficiary in lump sum or settlement option under the 5-year rule.* If beneficiary is owner's surviving spouse, he or she may continue the contract. |
| Joint spousal | Individual or joint | Both owners | Death benefit paid to beneficiary in lump sum or settlement option under the 5-year rule.* |
| Joint spousal | Individual or joint | 1 owner | Death benefit paid to joint owner in lump sum or settlement under the 5-year rule.* Spouse, as joint owner, may elect to continue the contract. |
| Joint spousal | Different joint individuals | 1 annuitant | Contract remains in force. |
| Joint spousal | Different joint individuals | Both annuitants | Owners become the annuitants. |
| Joint spousal | Different individual | Annuitant | Owners become the annuitants. |
| Trust or corporation | Individual or joint | 1 annuitant | Death benefit paid to beneficiary in lump sum or settlement option under the 5-year rule.* If beneficiary is a trust holding this contract solely for the benefit of the descendent's spouse, the trust may continue the contract for the benefit of the surviving spouse. if the trust or corporation is the beneficiary, the death benefit must be paid as a lump sum within one year. |

# Orderly Affairs

# Should You Retire Early?
# What You Need to Know About
# Social Security

*"When your outgo exceeds your income, your upkeep becomes your downfall."*

- Ken A. Loyall

Thinking about retirement can prompt pleasant fantasies about what you will do with all that free time:

- Sleep late every day
- Go fishing
- Do all those home projects that have been put off for years
- Travel
- Read
- Do volunteer work.

If you are not sure how you will make ends meet it can also be a confusing and frightening prospect. That is why it is critical that you make the most of your time until retirement and use your resources wisely by starting your planning now.

One of the basic building blocks of retirement income for most people is Social Security. While this alone is unlikely to meet your needs (consider that in 2001, the average monthly Social Security payment was $846), you still need to make some decisions about this important source of retirement income.

The biggest decision is whether to wait until you are 65 (or, if you were born in 1960 or later, 67) to start drawing Social Security in order to get the maximum amount. If you start earlier, you commit yourself to a reduced amount (as of 2002, 20% less if you retire at 62 but that will rise to 30%) for the rest of your lifetime.

There are some strong arguments for retiring early and drawing reduced benefits. One obvious one would be if you have ample resources and the amount of Social Security you draw isn't critical to your lifestyle, then you may simply prefer to retire early and get a

# Social Security Full Retirement and Reductions By Age

No Matter what your full retirement age is, you may start receiving benefits as early as age 62.

| Year of Birth | Full Retirement Age | Age 62 Reduction Months | Monthly % Reduction | Total % Reduction |
|---|---|---|---|---|
| 1937 or earlier | 65 | 36 | .555 | 20.00 |
| 1938 | 65 and 2 months | 38 | .548 | 20.83 |
| 1939 | 65 and 4 months | 40 | .541 | 21.67 |
| 1940 | 65 and 6 months | 42 | .535 | 22.50 |
| 1941 | 65 and 8 months | 44 | .530 | 23.33 |
| 1942 | 65 and 10 months | 46 | .525 | 24.17 |
| 1943-1954 | 66 | 48 | .520 | 25.00 |
| 1955 | 66 and 2 months | 50 | .516 | 25.84 |
| 1956 | 66 and 4 months | 52 | .512 | 26.66 |
| 1957 | 65 and 6 months | 54 | .509 | 27.50 |
| 1958 | 66 and 8 months | 56 | .505 | 28.33 |
| 1959 | 66 and 10 months | 58 | .502 | 29.17 |
| 1960 and later | 67 | 60 | .500 | 30.00 |

You can also retire at any time between age 62 and full retirement age. However, if you start at one of these early ages, your benefits are reduced a fraction of a percent for each month before your full retirement age.

head start on your tan.

Consider the benefit you receive from drawing Social Security just three years early. If you wait until 65, it will take almost 18 years to catch up to the total amount drawn by someone who retired at 62 (ignoring income tax considerations). Given the average life expectancy of Americans, retirees may not survive long enough to reach that catch-up point. Still, this must be weighed against the fact that the amount you receive each month is less than if you wait. This may be particularly important if your cash flow requirements require every possible dollar after retirement.

You should also bear in mind that by waiting to retire until 65 you continue to earn full income for an extra three years. Not only does this put more money in your pocket in the short term, it gives you a higher Social Security payout at retirement, and the cost-of-living increases will also be based on that higher amount.

You should also consider the tax implications of your choice. You are well advised to check with your tax and/or financial advisor when choosing a retirement strategy.

*Other Considerations*

Should you work part-time after you start to draw Social Security? The answer is: it depends. If you are 65 or older, there is no longer any penalty for earning extra money. If you are under 65, however, and you make more than $11,280 a year, you lose a full 50% of your Social Security income (as of 2002).

Another consideration is that Social Security provides more than just retirement income. If you become totally disabled and are unable to work prior to retirement age, then you can draw benefits. (Note that this is very difficult to be approved for, and may reduce other benefits.) There is also a provision for payments to aid any children you may have under the age of 18 in this case.

Note that if you receive a public pension that is outside the Social Security system, even if you earned full Social Security benefits from other employment, you may not be able to collect it when the time comes. If you are in this category (as many teachers are), ask your financial advisor about the Government Pension Offset and the Windfall Elimination Provision of the Social Security Law.

For more information, go to www.nea.org/lac/socsec.

# Medicare, Medicaid and Medi-Cal

*"It is not wealth one asks for, but just enough to preserve one's dignity, to work unhampered...to be independent."*
- W. Somerset Maugham

Y ou probably know that there is a government program to take care of medical expenses after you reach 65 but it is unlikely that you know exactly what it will - and won't - cover.

In fact, there are many services that the program does not cover. Now, not when you are sick, is the time to find out about your options so that you have adequate protection later.

ROBERT and LYNN

Robert was a retired surgeon with Medicare insurance when he required heart surgery. One week after the surgery, he was transferred to a skilled nursing facility (SNF) for physical therapy and other rehabilitation services. His Medicare caseworker kept close tabs on his recovery. As soon as the caseworker was informed that Robert was not responding to the physical therapy she told his wife Lynn that Medicare would no longer pay the costs of the SNF. (Medicare rules require that patients be improving in order to continue receiving benefits).

Lynn had no idea what to do. Robert had always handled all of the family's financial matters. She felt confused and helpless. She sat staring at the bills piling up on her table day after day. Seventy-four days after he entered the SNF, Robert died.

By then, the medical and nursing home bills totalled $77,000. Lynn eventually paid all of the bills but it consumed a third of her assets. Upon Robert's death, she also lost some pension benefits and Social Security income. With her reduced resources, Lynn was forced to seriously curtail her spending, which resulted in a very meager lifestyle.

Good Medicare supplementary insurance and long-term care coverage would have paid most of Robert's SNF expenses. It also would have given Lynn more to live on and less to worry about as she faced the last days of Robert's life and her future alone.

Most of us assume that our medical insurance will cover all of our health needs, but most plans do not cover the many levels of nursing or home care. For instance, many policies cover home care in a limited way but will not cover a home health aide. Most Health Management Organizations (HMO) contract with groups of physicians called Independent Physician Associations (IPA). The IPA contracts for skilled nursing and home health care. Depending upon the organization to which your doctor belongs, you may have excellent benefits or you may have none at all.

Some IPAs have patient liaison personnel, called case managers, who make sure that their patients get the level of care they need. They know that in the end, this will actually save money by avoiding unnecessary readmission to the hospital. Other organizations are less accommodating. These policies are especially important for the Medicare HMOs that so many seniors are now joining.

Check your health insurance policy to see if even the most basic home health care services and skilled nursing services are covered. None of these policies, including Medicare and "Medigap" plans, cover either custodial or protracted home and SNF care for any length of time.

*What are Medicare, Medicaid and Medi-Cal?*

Medicare is a federal medical insurance program provided to all Americans and legal residents age 65 and older. The same benefits are provided to everyone, regardless of income or assets. It also provides services to younger people with certain disabilities, and people with permanent kidney failure who need dialysis.

Both Medicaid and Medi-Cal are for those with meager resources. Medicaid is the federal arm of the program that pays some medical and assisted-living expenses and for certain types of long-term care.

Medi-Cal is California's version of Medicaid. To qualify for Medi-Cal benefits, you cannot have more than $2,000 in non-exempt assets and $35 per month in disposable income, as of 2002.

If you are reading this book, it is more than likely because you plan to have a financially comfortable life, at least in retirement. For that reason, we will concentrate on what Medicare covers (and, conversely, what it does not cover). Long term care benefits under Medicaid and Medi-Cal are so restrictive in terms of qualifying for the benefits that it is inapplicable in the vast majority of cases. It is, for all intents and purposes, unavailable to all but the most impoverished individuals.

*There are two parts of Medicare*

**Part A**
Hospital Insurance, which helps pay for medically necessary in-patient care in a hospital, a SNF or a psychiatric hospital and for hospice and home health care.

Medicare Part A is financed through the Social Security payroll tax paid by workers and their employers and the Self-Employment Tax paid by self-employed people. You do not have to pay a monthly premium for Part A if you or your spouse worked in Medicare-covered employment for at least ten years, you are at least 65 years old and you are a citizen or permanent resident of the United States. Certain younger disabled people and those with ESRD (End-Stage Renal Disease, which is permanent kidney failure and requires dialysis) also qualify for premium-free Part A benefits. If you do not qualify for premium-free Part A, you may buy it if you are at least 65 and meet certain other requirements.

## Part B

Medical Insurance, which helps pay for medically necessary physician services, outpatient hospital care and other medical services and supplies not covered by Part A. Both Parts A and B have deductibles and co-payments while Part A has benefit limitations as well.

Everyone who enrolls in Medicare Part B must pay a premium ($54 per month in 2002). Most enrollees have it deducted from their monthly Social Security checks. You are automatically enrolled in Part B when you become eligible for premium-free Part A, unless you state that you don't want it. Even if you do not qualify for premium-free Part A, you can usually buy Part B if you are 65 or older.

*What Medicare Covers*

Medicare covers up to 100 days of skilled nursing care needed within 30 days after a hospitalization of at least three days. The first 20 days are covered 100%; days 21 through 100 require a co-payment, as of spring 2002, of $101.50 per day. After 100 days, Medicare pays nothing and you must pay privately.

Medicare separates long-term care into "skilled" and "non-skilled". It pays only for services defined as skilled care, whether they are provided in a nursing facility or at home. Skilled or sub-acute nursing care must be serious enough that the services are provided or supervised by a licensed nurse (RN). SNFs must provide 24-hour nursing services and employ a nurse at least eight hours per day, seven days a week, to qualify. Any services that can be provided by a licensed practical nurse (LPN) or an aide are not considered skilled care, even if the individual needs them full-time or even if they are provided in a nursing home. Medicare also does not pay for chronic conditions. Patients must be improving for Medicare to continue payment.

Medicare defines "skilled care" to include IVs, regular muscular injections, tube feeding, physical therapy, speech therapy, continuous oxygen, treatment of deep skin lesions, suctioning, or close monitoring 24 hours a day.

Hospitals are paid by Medicare through a system known as DRGs (diagnostic related groups). Simply stated, this means that the hospital gets paid a set amount depending upon the diagnosis, not by the services it provides. Therefore, the shorter the stay or the less expensive the treatment that is provided, the more money the hospital makes. Hospitals, then, have little incentive to provide Medicare patients with exceptional care.

If your hospital stay is less than three days, there is no coverage at all under Medicare for any SNF care that may be required thereafter. Just staying in the hospital for three days is not enough, however. Medicare must certify that the stay was medically necessary and not just prolonged to cover the three-day requirement. Currently, Medicare is sporadic in checking to see if these criteria are met, but this will change as the need to stretch scarce resources increases.

Many patients go for "skilled rehabilitation" to strengthen them before they go home. Once skilled needs have been met and the patient can be managed at home, or at a lesser level of care, the Medicare and Medigap supplementary policy or private health insurance coverage ends.

This may happen long before the patient and family feel the patient is ready. Rarely has the patient reached a pre-illness functioning level when discharged from the hospital. Skilled nursing is provided for up to 100 days, but more recently persons requiring skilled care have received only about 11 days of care under the fully-paid Medicare program before they are discharged.

Once this coverage ends, the patient and family are left with having to pay for long-term care indefinitely. This can be as much as $6,000 per month, or even more, paid out of personal assets. Eventually, after you deplete almost your entire life savings, Medicaid will cover your basic needs. Not many first-class facilities accept Medicaid patients, although many nursing homes will allow a resident to convert to Medicaid when the patient's resources are sufficiently depleted. Typically, if you are readmitted to the hospital for more than ten days, however, your spot in the nursing home is no longer assured. You may end up being placed in a different facility after discharge from the hospital a second time.

Here is a summary list of benefits and coverage for Medicare:

## Medicare Part A
- Subject to deductibles, co-insurance payments, and benefit limitations
- Inpatient hospital care (hospital charges only; costs for physicians, surgeons or anesthesiologist are covered by Medicare Part B)
- Skilled nursing care in a SNF (up to 100 days)
- Medically necessary home health care (skilled care only)
- Hospice care
- Blood transfusions

## Medicare Part B
- Is voluntary
- Physician services
- Outpatient hospital care
- Surgical services and supplies
- Physical and speech therapy
- Ambulance transportation
- Diagnostic tests
- Durable medical equipment
- Prosthetic devices
- Blood transfusions

*Care at Home*

If you need care in your home, Medicare may pay some of your expenses, but you must meet certain requirements. You must be homebound requiring skilled nursing or rehabilitative services.

*Medigap Insurance*

Medigap insurance is designed to supplement Medicare's benefits. These policies are sold by private insurance companies and are regulated by federal and state law. The medical plan must be clearly identified as Medicare supplemental insurance and it must provide specific benefits that help fill the gaps in your Medicare coverage. Other kinds of insurance may help you with out-of-pocket healthcare costs but they do not qualify as Medigap plans.

There are ten standard Medigap insurance policies. (For more information see the Health Care Financing Administration publication "2001 Guide to Health Insurance for People with Medicare".)

You can now see why Medicare is only a limited part of the picture in ensuring that your medical needs are covered.

If you would like more information about these issues, please see the list of resources at the back of this book.

# Medicare Supplement Insurance: Medigap

Medicare supplement insurance can be sold in only ten standard plans. This chart shows the benefits included in each plan.

| A | B | C | D | E | F | G | H | I | J |
|---|---|---|---|---|---|---|---|---|---|
| Basic Benefits | Basic Benefits | Basic Benefits | Basic Benefits | Basic Benefits | Basic Benefits | Basic Benefits | Basic Benefits | Basic Benefits | Basic Benefits |
|  |  | Skilled Nursing Co-Insurance | Skilled Nursing Co-Insurance | Skilled Nursing Co-Insurance | Skilled Nursing Co-Insurance | Skilled Nursing Co-Insurance | Skilled Nursing Co-Insurance | Skilled Nursing Co-Insurance | Skilled Nursing Co Insurance |
|  | Part A Deductible | Part A Deductible | Part A Deductible | Part A Deductible | Part A Deductible | Part A Deductible | Part A Deductible | Part A Deductible | Part A Deductible |
|  |  | Part B Deductible |  |  | Part B Deductible |  |  |  | Part B Deductible |
|  |  |  |  |  | Part B Excess (100%) | Part B Excess (80%) |  | Part B Excess (100%) | Part B Excess (100%) |
|  |  | Foreign Travel Emergency | Foreign Travel Emergency | Foreign Travel Emergency | Foreign Travel Emergency | Foreign Travel Emergency | Foreign Travel Emergency | Foreign Travel Emergency | Foreign Travel Emergency |
|  |  |  | At-Home Recovery |  |  | At-Home Recovery |  | At-Home Recovery | At-Home Recovery |
|  |  |  |  |  |  |  | Basic Drugs $1,250 limit | Basic Drugs $1,250 limit | Ext. Drugs $1,250 limit |
|  |  |  |  | Preventive Care |  |  |  |  | Preventive Care |

*Basic Benefits (included in all plans): Hospitalization - Part A coinsurance plus coverage for 365 days after Medicare ends. Medical Expenses- Part B coinsurance (generally 20% of Medicare Approved expenses). Blood - First three pints each year.*

# How to Choose a Financial Advisor

"To profit from receiving good advice requires more wisdom than to give it."

- John Churton Collins

You are reading this book because you are a concerned individual who wants more information in order to control your financial destiny. Information in the world of financial matters is constantly changing. As tax laws change and as the economy grows more complex, no one individual can be expected to master financial matters without a full time commitment to ongoing training, education and the desire and ability to specialize in the field. That is why there are financial advisors. It is their job to be the experts and to stay current on these matters.

A financial planner has a broad knowledge of areas such as tax planning, investments, and estate planning, but is unlikely to be the professional you require for specific help in each of these areas. Rather the financial planner can coordinate your financial affairs between your accountant, insurance agent, stock broker, and estate lawyer. The broad expertise that a professional financial planner possesses will help insure that your financial goals are met and that all areas of your financial life are reviewed.

How do you know that an advisor has the knowledge he or she needs to do a good job advising you? One of the hallmarks of a professional is accreditation by a recognized professional association. This means the advisor has completed required courses and has been tested on his knowledge. Additionally, many times there are on-going educational requirements that the planner must meet in order to maintain accreditation.

Nevertheless, your role does not end by handing over your finances to someone with credentials. Your financial advisor's primary function, in fact, should be to educate YOU.

What other information helps you select the right financial advisor/planner? Here are some guidelines to consider when choosing among professionals (adapted from the Certified Financial Planner Board of Standards):

## What experience does the advisor have?

Find out how long the advisor has been in practice and the number and types of companies with which the advisor has been associated. Ask the advisor to briefly describe his work experience and how it relates to his current practice. Choose a financial planner who has a minimum of three years experience counseling individuals on their financial needs.

## What are the advisor's qualifications?

Many individuals with very differing backgrounds and training use the term "financial planner". Ask the planner what qualifies him to offer financial planning advice and whether he holds a financial planning designation such as the Certified Financial Planner mark. Look for a planner who has proven experience in financial planning topics such as insurance, tax planning, investments, estate planning or retirement planning. Determine what steps the planner takes to stay current with changes and developments in the financial planning field. If the planner holds a financial planning designation, check on his/her background with the CFP Board or other relevant professional organizations.

## What services does the advisor offer?

The services a financial planner offers depend on a number of factors including credentials, licenses and areas of expertise. Financial planners cannot sell insurance or securities products such as mutual funds or stocks without the proper licenses. Nor may they give investment advice unless registered with state or federal authorities.

Some planners offer financial planning advice on a range of topics but do not sell financial products. Others may provide advice only in specific areas such as estate planning or on tax matters.

### What is the advisor's approach to financial planning?

Ask the financial planner about the type of clients and financial situations he typically likes to work with. Some planners prefer to develop one plan by bringing together all of your financial goals. Others provide advice on specific areas, as needed. Make sure the planner's viewpoint on investing is not too cautious or overly aggressive for you. Some planners require you to have a certain net worth before offering services. Find out if the planner will carry out the financial recommendations developed for you or refer you to others who will do so.

### Will that advisor be the only person working with you?

The financial planner may work with you himself, or have others in the office to assist you. You may want to meet everyone who will be working with you. If the planner works with professionals outside his own practice (such as attorneys, insurance agents or tax specialists) to develop or carry out financial planning recommendations, have him provide you with their names and a description of their training and experience.

### How will you pay for the advisor's services?

As part of your financial planning agreement, the financial planner should clearly tell you in writing how he will be paid for the services to be provided. Planners can be paid in several ways:

- A salary paid by the company for which the planner works. The planner's employer receives payment from you or others, either in fees or commissions, in order to pay the planner's salary.

- Fees based on an hourly rate, a flat rate, or on a percentage of your assets and/or income.

- Commissions paid by a third party from the products sold to you to carry out the financial planning recommendations. Commissions are usually a percentage of the amount you invest in a financial product.

- A combination of fees and commissions whereby fees are charged for the amount of work done to develop financial planning recommendations and commissions are received from any products sold.

**How much does the advisor typically charge?**

While the amount you pay the planner will depend on your particular needs, the financial planner should be able to provide you with an estimate of possible costs based on the work to be performed. Such costs would include the planner's hourly rates or flat fees or the percentage he would receive as commission on products you may purchase as part of the financial planning recommendations.

**Could anyone other than you benefit from the advisor's recommendations?**

Some business relationships or partnerships that a planner has could affect the planner's professional judgment in working with you, possibly inhibiting the planner from acting in your best interest.

**Has the advisor ever been publicly disciplined for any unlawful or unethical actions in his professional career?**

Several government and professional regulatory organizations, such as the National Association of Securities Dealers (NASD), your state insurance and securities departments, and the CFP Board keep records on the disciplinary history of financial planners and advisers. Ask what organizations the planner is regulated by, and contact these groups to conduct a background check. All financial planners who have registered as investment advisers with the Securities and Exchange Commission, or state securities agencies, or who are associated with a company that is registered as an investment adviser must be able to provide you with a disclosure form called Form ADV or the state equivalent of that form.

## Can you have it in writing?

Ask the planner to provide you with a written agreement that details the services that will be provided. Keep this document in your files for future reference.

# Orderly Affairs

# *Living Trusts*

*"What you leave at your death let it be without controversy, else the lawyers will be your heirs."*

— F. Osborn

## JOAN

Joan, 62 years of age, sought advice from her attorney to determine what course of action she should take regarding having a living trust or a will drafted.

For Joan, a living trust fulfilled several needs. Since she was single, she was concerned about the management of her assets if she became incapacitated. By selecting a trusted advisor and long-time friend as her trustee, she knew that in the event that she was unable to take care of her own assets, her advisor would be able to make these critical decisions for her.

Joan observed to her attorney that she probably could have done the trust planning that took approximately four hours to complete, if she had five years to study both federal and state tax law, investment planning, and insurance rules and regulations. She also knew she would have needed to rely on the personal experience of friends and associates to feel comfortable and to be sure she had not missed important parts in the estate planning process. Seeking the advice of a trusted advisor gave her peace of mind that she had not missed any critical steps.

*Living Trust or Will? When is each of these documents used?*

**Will:**
One of the better definitions for a will is that it is simply a letter to a judge. A will has no legal effect while you are living; it takes effect only when you die. A will then needs to be presented to a judge, through a legal proceeding called a probate, to be interpreted. If you die without a will, the laws of the state in which you reside at time

of death control who gets the assets from your estate. If you live in the western United States and you are married, your estate will more than likely fall under the community property rules. Most other parts of the country adhere to a different set of rules. Without a will, your property may well go to relatives you might not want to receive it.

## Living Trust:

A living trust is a document in which the "trustor" or "settlor" transfers her property into the living trust. Typically, the trustor is also the trustee of her own trust, as long as she is able to manage her own assets. Upon her incapacity or her death, a successor trustee steps in to carry out the trustor/settlor's wishes contained in the living trust document.

*What are the advantages of a living trust?*

• A living trust avoids probate, which is both time-consuming and expensive. For example, in Joan's case, her $2.5 million estate would have to pay out approximately $35,000 in legal fees plus another $35,000 in administrative fees for an executor to administer the estate in probate. (State law typically sets both the attorney's fee and executor's fee where the probate occurs.) With a living trust, most of these fees are avoidable, or greatly reduced.

• A living trust can provide for immediate distributions to beneficiaries without the necessity of probate court review or approval. A probate, on the other hand, will take a minimum of several months to complete. This means that distributions to heirs will be delayed.

• A living trust is strictly a private document, where the value of the estate does not need to become a matter of public record. Under the probate process, on the other hand, all assets need to be inventoried, with the inventory being filed with the court. Any privacy as to the value of the estate is, therefore, lost.

- A living trust works for you while you are alive. If you become incapacitated, your designated successor trustee can step in and manage your assets. Without a living trust or other planning, the mechanism to manage your assets in the event of your incapacity is a "living" probate, or "conservatorship". Once again, the conservatorship becomes a matter of public record as well as the inventory and value of your assets.

Missed steps can certainly mean paying additional and sometimes substantial income and estate taxes, either during your lifetime or at death. Most importantly, after your death, errors can mean denying those you care about the benefits and assets that you have worked your whole life to accumulate.

Many people incorrectly assume that a will automatically sets up the proper transfer of assets to beneficiaries and avoids probate expenses for the balance of the estate. In most cases, nothing could be further from the truth. The following vehicles normally bypass probate, with a valid will:

- Life and annuity insurance policies, IRA and pension accounts, and other accounts with proper beneficiary designations;

- Property given as a gift to another person, property that has been transferred by trust document, and property held in joint tenancy (probate still applies at the death of the surviving joint tenant). Joint tenancy should be used with great caution. For example, under joint tenancy, it is possible to unintentionally disinherit a child from a prior marriage, since joint tenancy will be given legal precedence over terms of a will. It happens frequently, and creates significant problems for potential heirs.

- If your estate is subject to probate, it will have to pay fees to attorneys (set by law at between 4% to 7% of the estate value), and extraordinary fees (charged by attorneys or specialists for extra services and approved by the probate court). There are also court costs that can run another 1% to 2%.

- Probate includes the process of closing the estate. It can lead to substantial delays (sometimes months or years) as various family and business issues are resolved. This can lead to serious additional costs and losses, especially if a business is left to flounder for lack of control and authority.

- Probate also opens the estate to public record and review, since all creditors of the estate must be given complete information about the estate's financial status.

When using a will or a living trust, it is important to remember that your estate will be subject to:

- Estate taxes: It is critical to remember that some or all of these taxes can be avoided by using credits, deductions, charitable bequests and various types of trusts.

- State inheritance taxes. This definitely requires legal and tax counsel since various states consider these taxes differently, including the use of matching credits to the federal taxation system. In some cases there is no exemption for transfer to the surviving spouse, and beneficiaries may also be taxed. Check with your local advisor on this issue.

- Generation-skipping transfer tax (GSTT): If it applies, it is a whopping flat 55% tax, in addition to the other income and estate taxes on any transfers made to certain named beneficiaries. These can include relatives, such as grandchildren, or other lineal heirs. Great care must be exercised with planning for this tax, since it is so onerous.

# Charitable Trusts

*"The true meaning of life is to plant trees under whose shade you do not expect to sit."*

- Nelson Henderson

The charitable remainder trust is rapidly becoming a favorite planning tool for clients because it can achieve extraordinary benefits for clients and their favorite charities. Congress has enacted laws that provide substantial tax benefits to those willing to make a deferred gift to charity. Specifically, a charitable remainder trust (CRT) can be designed to pay income for life to the donor, their spouse, their children or even non-family members. Whatever is left over after the passing of the beneficiary goes to the charity designated by the trust. By agreeing to make this deferred gift, the donor is given a variety of tax incentives, which include:

- A current income-tax deduction for a charitable gift.

- The ability to sell the asset within the trust and not pay any capital gains tax.

- An income for life or other set period of time, based upon a percentage of the remainder value of whatever is in the trust, computed on an annual basis at a percentage predetermined by the donor.

- Removal of the asset from the donor's estate for estate tax purposes.

- The right to change the charitable beneficiary in the future.

- The right to select a trustee to manage the assets and/or the right of the trust owner to act as trustee personally.

When you add up the fact that the donor (1) will not pay capital gains tax, (2) will not pay estate tax and (3) will receive a charitable deduction for the deferred gift, the donor may well be better off utilizing a charitable trust to sell stock, real estate or any other substantially appreciated assets versus selling the assets conventionally and receiving proceeds net of taxes.

This technique, until recently, was utilized almost exclusively by very wealthy clients but is now becoming more commonly used by anyone who has substantially appreciated assets that are subject to capital gains taxes.

MR. and MRS. ENGEL

In 1992, the Engels sought advice from their attorney regarding the best way to handle a real estate transaction. They had purchased a trailer park in 1966 for approximately $100,000. Now, the trailer park was worth $2 million. Mr. and Mrs. Engel were 61 and 58 years old, respectively, and were ready to retire. They also had no children or close relatives to leave this valuable asset.

Their goals were to:

• Sell the trailer park;
• Reduce or eliminate any capital gains taxes on the sale;
• Provide themselves with an income for the rest of their lives; and
• Leave money to charity.

If Mr. and Mrs. Engel had simply sold their real estate outright, the combined federal and California capital gains tax would have amounted to around 37% of $1.9 million, or approximately $700,000 in tax. This would have left only $1.3 million to be invested for their retirement. Assuming a 7% annual rate of return on their investment, this would provide them with $91,000 a year in income. Alternatively, if they wanted to bequeath the proceeds to friends or family, because they were in a 50% federal estate-tax bracket at the time, this would have left only about half, or $650,000, to go to their heirs.

By using a charitable remainder trust, there was no tax to pay upon the sale of the trailer park. The amount available to be invested was a full $2 million. At a 7% annual rate of return, this amounts to $140,000 per year to retire on, or a $49,000-per-year difference!

In addition, Mr. and Mrs. Engel received a charitable deduction of approximately $300,000. The deduction was used to offset up to 30% of their adjusted gross income on an annual basis. (What isn't used in the current year can be carried over and used over the next five years.) Given the Engels' tax bracket, the benefit of this deduction over the next five years amounted to an additional $140,000 after tax.

Had they wanted to, Mr. and Mrs. Engel could have used the $140,000 in tax savings to buy a "second-to-die" life insurance policy. A second-to-die policy only pays insurance proceeds on the death of the second spouse. That policy, which could be positioned outside of the Engels' taxable estate, could have easily funded a $2 million death benefit to be paid to any relatives or friends they might have chosen.

Mr. and Mrs. Engel decided they wanted to be their own trustees. They selected four local charities, and maintained the right to revoke the gifts to those charities in case they became unhappy about the way the charities were being run.

In the end, Mr. and Mrs. Engel received the following benefits by utilizing a charitable trust versus simply selling the trailer park and paying all of the taxes:

- $49,000 more per year in current income;
- A tax benefit worth $140,000 in after-tax dollars;
- Control over the trust property, because they decided to be the trustees of their own trust;

- The opportunity to use the $140,000 to replace the asset for a full $2 million outside of their taxable estate if they had chosen to; and
- A gift of $2 million to their favorite charities from the charitable trust upon the death of the second one of them.

*When is a Charitable Trust most useful?*

The critical issue is tax liability, along with the desire to leave money to charity. Other issues to consider:

- Has the asset that you would like to sell substantially appreciated over time so that it would generate a large capital gains tax?

# Charitable Remainder Unitrust

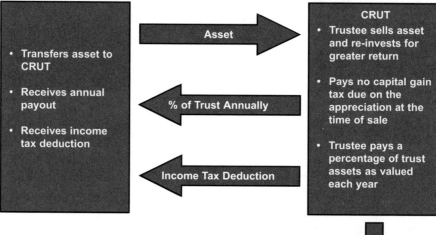

- Transfers asset to CRUT
- Receives annual payout
- Receives income tax deduction

**Asset**

**% of Trust Annually**

**Income Tax Deduction**

CRUT
- Trustee sells asset and re-invests for greater return
- Pays no capital gain tax due on the appreciation at the time of sale
- Trustee pays a percentage of trust assets as valued each year

After the beneficiary is deceased remaining trust assets pass to the charity

- Receive any asset remaining in the trust when the beneficiary is deceased

- Can you live on the income generated from your investments and not need to tap the principal?

Many charities are more than happy to help run projections for clients to show them the benefits of this type of planning. Obviously, it is important to consult with your tax advisor with regard to the strategy utilized.

# Orderly Affairs

# *Other Special Types of Trusts*

*"Most people think more about creating an estate than conserving an estate."*

- Brian D. Heckert

After reading the chapter on Living Trusts, you may have questions on other types of trusts not mentioned. There are, in fact, many types of trusts available that can be used to accomplish important personal and tax objectives. Some of these special types of trusts are listed below. This list is not meant to be all-inclusive, nor is it meant to be a thorough description of when and how these trusts are used.

Some trusts are "revocable". This means that the trust can be changed or amended after it has been funded. If a trust cannot be changed, it is termed "irrevocable" or "not-available".

*Revocable Trust Utilizing an A/B (Bypass) Trust*

Married couples may utilize this type of trust. Upon the death of the first spouse, a marital deduction for federal estate-tax purposes allows for a complete transfer of all assets to the surviving spouse without any federal estate-taxes payable (certain unintended consequences can occur if careful planning isn't done, however).

In addition to a marital deduction, there is also an estate-tax provision that currently allows for a maximum exemption of $1,000,000 per person. An A/B or "bypass" trust, properly created at the first spouse's death, preserves the first spouse's $1,000,000 exemption. This exemption amount is currently scheduled to increase through 2010.

*Irrevocable Life Insurance Trust*

Most people are not aware that life insurance proceeds can be subject to estate tax. A simple technique to avoid this problem is to have the policy owned from inception by an irrevocable life insurance trust, or to transfer policy ownership to an insurance trust. Upon the death of the insured, the proceeds from the policy can pass to the beneficiaries of the insurance policy (and trust) estate tax-free. If an existing policy is transferred into an insurance trust, you must survive three years after transfer to prevent the proceeds from being taxed inside your estate, according to IRS rules.

*Dynasty Trust*

A dynasty trust is a special type of irrevocable life insurance trust that is used to avoid estate taxes for successive generations on life insurance policies held within this trust. Not only can estate taxes be avoided, but the dreaded generation-skipping transfer tax can be avoided, as well, in passing substantial wealth to grandchildren and great-grandchildren.

*QTIP Trust (Qualified Terminable Interest Property Trust)*

Typically, this trust is used to protect assets for children of a prior marriage. It allows the creator of the trust to restrict the surviving spouse's ability to access trust assets, so as to protect those assets until the death of the surviving spouse. Income is provided to the surviving spouse while he or she is living, but the trust principal is conserved for the creator's children at the death of the second spouse.

As you can see from the preceding chapters, trusts provide an excellent and unique way to control the disposition of assets upon death and can be a very effective tax-planning vehicle, as well. Since laws affecting estate planning frequently change, you are encouraged to discuss these and other options with your financial advisor and attorney.

# How to Build a Real Estate Empire

*"The fortunate circumstances of our lives are generally found, at last, to be of our own producing."*
                                        - Goldsmith

Sometimes you have money you didn't know you had. No, not a forgotten bank account in some faraway hamlet, or an unknown inheritance from fourth-cousin Gertrude, twice removed.

If you have a cash value life insurance policy or if you own your own business, you may have borrowing power or cash outright that you can use to invest in something else.

That is precisely how the people in the following stories began their "real estate empires".

MATT and HELEN

Back in the early 1980s, Matt and Helen started a business out of their garage at home doing high-quality printing. As the business grew, they rented increasing space in various other locations until the late 1980s.

In 1988, they took out life insurance policies on themselves. They also took out cash-value life insurance policies on their two children who were working in the business to create a retirement plan for them, even though they were still young people. After paying for the policies for a number of years, they found that they could borrow cash from the policies, as well as borrow on their home equity. With that money, they bought an office building. They rented out part of it to other tenants, and used the balance of the building for their own business.

Over the years they watched the value of the building increase from the $1.2 million they originally paid to a current value of $8 million.

In addition, they were able to buy two houses to rent out, which have now appreciated by another $1 million. They are ready to start a very comfortable and well-earned retirement, with considerable income from their real estate empire.

BERNARD

Bernard was an engineer with a telephone company. During his years there, he developed an interest in real estate investments and bought his first investment property. He eventually obtained a real estate license in his spare time and gradually built his real estate business and reputation. Later, he decided to become a real estate broker, by which time, he was selling enough property to quit the phone company. He built his own business by selling full-time to other buyers while continuing to buy real estate for his own portfolio. The income his wife earned (also at the same company) made the down payments!

Bernard and his wife managed the properties as they built a real estate empire. He also created a profit-sharing plan for his real estate business in which he was able to provide financing to homebuyers, many of them also real estate investors. In time, he was able to offer private mortgages to clients and the public, further increasing his real estate income while adding to the value of his profit-sharing plan. Eventually, he was able to retire in his 50s. He and his wife continue to manage and own their real estate investments. He also continues to invest his profit-sharing plan in private mortgages.

Along the way, Bernard and his wife turned their original real estate investment property into a charitable remainder trust, benefiting their favorite charities and adding to their lifetime income. This also eliminated the otherwise large capital gains tax liability and gave themselves a charitable deduction to boot!

JUSTIN

Justin's father started a franchise. His parents ran the business for more than 25 years, and when they were ready to retire, Justin and his sister Laura, who had been employees of the business for many years, agreed to buy the franchise over a ten-year period.

During the time that Justin and Laura owned the business, they bought real estate for their business operation on three different occasions, each time "moving up" in value as the business grew in size. They started with a single location that was worth $200,000 and now own a large building worth many times that amount. The business went from occupying a space of approximately 2,000 square feet to over 50,000 square feet. Justin and Laura owned the buildings personally, while the business paid them rent for use of the space.

In 1999 they sold the business to a publicly traded company. Justin and Laura each received stock on a tax-free basis in exchange for their business. As part of the transaction, the buyer agreed to lease their buildings.

By reinvesting the proceeds from their business, Justin and Laura were able to purchase commercial property that is now worth many millions of dollars. The alternative, of course, was for the business to continue to "rent" space each year without any equity buildup. Justin and Laura were able to position themselves to participate in the rapid appreciation in real estate that occurred in their area, a hub of the high-tech industry.

In summary, Justin and Laura purchased the business from their parents for $2 million in 1987. They sold the business in 1997 for $6 million on a tax-free basis. This netted them a tidy $4 million profit. However, what is even more impressive is that by utilizing resources that would normally go out in rent, or "down the drain", they were able to parlay their real estate holdings from an initial value of $200,000 to approximately $5 million in 1997 (when they sold the business).

Justin and Laura positioned themselves to take advantage of a rapidly rising real estate market by deciding to be their own landlords. By purchasing property where their business was located and paying themselves rent to cover the mortgage on the real estate, they gave themselves the opportunity to participate in capital appreciation in real estate that they would never have otherwise been able to afford.

# Being In Business: From Getting In To Getting Out

*"Success in business requires training and discipline and hard work. But if you're not frightened by these things, the opportunities are just as great today as they ever were."*
- David Rockefeller

Whether you own your own company or have simply dreamed of one day being your own boss, understanding the benefits -- and risks -- of running your own business is critical to your financial well being.

This is especially true in this era of corporate downsizing and lack of job security. When jobs can disappear as quickly as yesterday's "dot-coms", many skilled employees are asking themselves if they shouldn't invest in their own future by being in business for themselves.

In the United States today, small businesses are creating about 99% of all the new jobs in the economy. Most entrepreneurs, however, are poorly informed about how to plan a business from beginning to end. This means, first and above all, having a clear understanding of how to make the business serve your own interests, rather than being a slave to the business you've created.

Companies were originally created as legal entities both as a means to generate wealth and to limit personal liability. What is one of the greatest advantages that help a company create wealth? Tax deductions! That is, a company earns its income and then deducts all of its legitimate expenses before tax is paid. As an individual, you can only do this under very specific situations and, most of the time, you pay taxes on all of your taxable earnings. Paying for expenses within the structure of a corporation can save as much as 30%, or more, of the cost of those expenses.

Of course, incorporating has benefits, above and beyond, just minimizing taxes. It also can be a key strategy in protecting your assets, especially in today's litigious atmosphere. Owning your own business means to always live with the possibility that, in spite of all your planning and hard work, your business could fail. Do you really want to put all of your personal assets at risk? For all these reasons, many entrepreneurs consider the incorporation of their business to be an important first step in their business venture.

Whether conducted within a corporation, or not, starting your own business many times comes down to turning something you are uniquely good at and qualified to do into a venture that can be profitable. In other cases, an unforeseen or new opportunity may arise and the business venture is launched once a sound business plan is put together. In still other cases, the business may result from a hobby or interest, as it did with Fernando.

## FERNANDO - *Turning a Hobby into a Living*

After successful stints in sales and personnel, Fernando became a stockbroker, eventually doing well enough to purchase a yacht, on which he frequently entertained clients. As a sideline, he started taking out paying clients, which paid for upkeep and insurance on the yacht. He then started hiring out his boat for weekend fishing parties as a means to earning extra income.

One day a prospective customer asked for a dinner cruise for 24 people. Although he had never done one before, Fernando hired a bartender and recruited his wife to cook. In four hours, they made more money than Fernando took in for 12 hours of fishing charters.

Within a year, Fernando and his wife had switched over entirely from fishing to lunch cruises. This was the birth of what is now a very successful tour boat business.

## FRED

Fred was a government employee earning a very good salary as an economist when he heard that his branch was going to be re-organized. At first Fred thought it was simply a bureaucratic exercise but he soon found out that his branch had been cut two positions. When the government offered an incentive of six months salary to anyone choosing to leave, Fred saw this as an opportunity to quit his government job and head out on his own.

His wife had been managing a home furnishings store during the previous two years. She and Fred decided that they would open a similar store across town using the $35,000 of their savings.

The couple prepared an impressive business plan and incorporated. By forming a corporation, they gave themselves the ability to decide when and how much salary to pay themselves, thereby being able to choose a strategy that minimized income taxes. Incorporation also enabled them to deduct more of their expenses, since much of their travel and entertaining was business-related. During those first few critical years, they took minimal salaries, keeping their personal income-tax liability low and keeping retained earnings within the company to fund its growth.

The couple soon expanded their operation from one to three stores. With the increased profits, they were now making more than they ever had as someone else's employees. Their business grew from their initial investment of $35,000 in 1987 to a value of $850,000 by 1995.

When they went into business, however, they never thought about how one or both of them would get out, and they had no agreement on how to do this. Unfortunately, the stress of the business eventually contributed to their decision to separate. Although the separation was amicable, between lawyers and accountant's fees, and tax consequences they hadn't planned for, the split cost them over $175,000.

How could they have avoided the financial hit they took? One way would have been through an ESOP (Employee Stock Ownership Plan). This is a trust to which the corporation makes annual tax-deductible contributions to employees' accounts. When the owner of a closely held corporation (one in which most of the voting stock is held by a few shareholders) eventually sells the business or retires, there is no capital gains tax on the sale of stock to an ESOP, provided that the ESOP owns at least 30% of the company immediately after the sale. We'll look at ESOPs in much greater detail in the next chapter.

DAVE

In 1983 Dave saw an opportunity to purchase a medical products business that he believed was not being well managed and needed active experienced ownership. Although it had an annual sales volume of $300,000, it had only three employees, and it was not turning a profit. Dave and his partner Jack, however, had little money with which to make an offer to buy the firm. They also had families to provide for, did not live where the business was located and had never successfully run a business by themselves. They only had experience in sales management of very large international corporations.

Dave and Jack presented a proposal to the owner, Sam, that each of them would put up $20,000 into a "working capital account". Dave and Jack would each own 50% of the business. The two would work with the old owner to make the company successful and, if they were not successful, they would hand over the $40,000 "working capital account" to Sam. If they succeeded, however, then Sam would get a percentage of the profits over a period of five years.

Dave and Jack pulled it off! They created a larger business going from $300,000 in yearly sales to more than $11,000,000 in sales per year. Pretax profits of more than $1,000,000 became the norm in later years, and they created jobs for 90 employees.

Later Dave decided to sell his half interest in the business for $2,500,000. With the proceeds, he invested in real estate and the securities markets and has not had a "job" for years, rather living off the income from his real estate and securities portfolios.

*What did Dave and Jack need to do to achieve Financial Freedom?*

- They needed to take a calculated risk based on their confidence in their abilities.

- They had to be willing to work very hard and very smart, not wasting precious time and resources on actions that would not lead to their success.

- They realized they needed to share the workload and use their strongest talents in different areas of the company.

- As they grew the business they constantly looked for ways to keep costs down, be innovative in the products and services they offered their customers.

- They hired the best people they could to meet customer requirements

Other possibilities that may have created even greater success:

- They could have planned ahead and structured a multi-year buyout strategy, taking into consideration the consequences of income and capital taxes on the sale proceeds, and minimized total taxes so Dave would have realized more net proceeds.

- They could have created a tax-free sale of the business by incorporating an Employee Stock Ownership Plan (ESOP), allowing for the business owners to buy each other out on a tax free or very favorable low tax basis, and for the employees to share in the growth of the business over time through increased value in their retirement accounts.

- They could have funded a buy-sell agreement that would allow the surviving owner to buy out the interest of the deceased or disabled employee/owner (if that had occurred).
- Other solutions might have encompassed Dave's family members buying into the business over time so they could enjoy growing the business to even greater success in the years ahead.

It's easy to see that there is more to getting into business than meets the eye. There is a lot to know about how to structure your company to best advantage, and the assistance of a good lawyer and accountant can be invaluable. Even before you talk with them, however, you should have the answers to the following questions worked out:

- How long do I want to be in this business?

- What do I want to achieve in my business?

- What kind of lifestyle do I want to live, and when?

- Are my personal assets protected if my business fails?

- What arrangements do I need to have in place between my partner and myself now?

- Am I indispensable?  If so, how am I going to change this, and when?

- What systems and documentation do I need to create to add value to my business?

- What is my strategy for staff training and retention?

- What do I need to do now to protect my business in case of illness or accident?

- How can I structure things now to maximize the eventual return I can get from the business?

- What am I uniquely exceptional at doing, and what things should I not do?

- What can I or should I delegate, and to whom?

By including these often overlooked items into your business plan (you <u>do</u> have a business plan, don't you?), you will be well ahead of the vast majority of entrepreneurs. You will also be on your way to ensuring your business provides you with maximum returns and value.

# Orderly Affairs

# Employee Stock Ownership Plans

*"There are always opportunities through which businessmen can profit handsomely if they will only recognize and seize them."*
- J. Paul Getty

In the wake of the Enron collapse, the largest and most controversial bankruptcy in U.S. history, qualified retirement plans have been receiving much more attention in the news media. These include retirement solutions such as 401(k)s, profit sharing plans, defined benefit plans, etc.

One qualified plan rarely referred to, however, is an employee stock ownership plan (commonly called ESOPs). ESOPs were created more than 50 years ago by the U.S. Congress as a means to encourage more ownership of small businesses by their employees. Today, ESOPs are common to more than 12,000 US businesses. An ESOP is a specialized type of defined contribution plan, and it has two distinct differences from other qualified plans. First, it can borrow money; and secondly, it can invest in the stock of the employer sponsoring the plan. These qualified plans must, and do, meet the requirements of the Department of Labor and the rules and regulations of the IRS and ERISA.

The primary benefit of an ESOP is that it allows for business owners to buy each other out on a tax-free basis, or at least a very low tax basis. It also allows employees to share in the growth of the business over time through increased value in their retirement accounts.

Here is how it works. An ESOP is a trust into which the company makes annual tax-deductible contributions (as of this writing, the maximum is 25% of eligible compensation before any 401(k) or Section 125 plan deferrals are made).

These contributions are allocated to individual employee accounts in the trust. Employees of a publicly traded company may sell their shares on the market. For a privately held firm, the company must buy back shares of any departing participant.

One benefit to the company is that the contributions to the plan are tax-deductible, thus increasing working capital to expand operations or to acquire new ones, and cash flow. It is also a big motivator for employees to share in the ownership and future of the business.

When the owner of a closely held company (one in which most of the voting stock is held by a few shareholders) eventually sells the business or retires, there is no capital gains tax on the sale of stock to an ESOP, provided that the ESOP owns at least 30% of the company right after the sale.

GEORGE

George, the owner of large trucking company in the Northeast, had twice tried to sell the company, each time for about $6 million, but each time the prospective buyer's financing fell through. Shortly after that, George's CPA talked him into starting an ESOP for his employees, although George was doubtful about the wisdom of doing so. He soon became a convert when he realized that he could sell a 30% interest in the company to the ESOP. Not only that, but the company was worth far more than the $6 million he had previously been offered, and he was able to have the ESOP pay him $4.5 million for only a 30% interest in the firm. He later sold four real estate parcels used for the trucking operations to the ESOP, which brought him another $4.5 million.

George assembled the employees one day to announce that the company had been sold. The announcement was met with deafening silence -- until he said it had been sold to the employees. After he explained the benefits to his workers, he got a standing ovation.

The best part? The entire $9 million George received from the sale to the ESOP was free of capital-gains tax, he still controlled the company, and his employees (now employee-owners) put their hearts into their contribution to the company's success.

There are various other benefits and protections associated with ESOPs:

- Should the company need funds to secure the buyout of the key shareholder(s), bank financing can be repaid with the interest and the principal both deductible, when properly structured.

- Employees may request their vested account portions at termination (within a reasonable settlement period with the plan), at disability, death, or when they retire.

- ESOPs can also have 401(k)s as an additional benefit for personal employee tax planning, and to meet specific savings goals.

The ability to sell your business on a tax favored basis, borrow money and deduct the repayment of principal and interest on a tax favorable basis, and still retain control until you are prepared to sell out completely, make ESOPs one of the most powerful tools of corporate finance. To receive your sales proceeds tax-free means more money for retirement, and for future generations to achieve their financial and family succession goals. The ability to transfer the business interest without tax makes the transaction truly unique, and allows families to draw substantial equity out of a growing business while maintaining a family interest for the future.

In summary, an ESOP is a defined contribution retirement plan in which:

- The company can make the contribution in stock or cash.

- Contributions are not taxed to the employee

- Dividends are deductible when properly passed through in cash.

- The buyout of the company owner can be accomplished in a private sale.

- The sale can be done on a tax-free basis if completed properly.
- The owner(s) can diversify their personal holdings for estate tax purposes.

- The sharing of ownership with employees in the plan creates a team spirit.

- The funds in an ESOP account can help to provide growth for the business.

- Forfeited benefits of departed employees are allocated to the accounts of active participants.

- The purchase of another business can be completed on a tax-free basis.

- The business can sell a division with an ESOP.

- Stock option plans can also be created with an ESOP.

It should be further noted that charitable deductions could be generated for the benefit of the business owner through the use of an ESOP in conjunction with a Charitable Trust. Life insurance, too, can be purchased on a pretax basis, and the death proceeds can be received tax-free, if properly designed in the ESOP plan.

*Appendices*

**Orderly Affairs**

## APPENDIX A:  Financial Planner Questionnaire

Planner Name:_____

Company:       _____

Address:       _____

Telephone:     _____

Date:          _____

1)      Do you have experience in providing advice on the topics below?  If yes, please indicate the number of years:

Retirement planning     _____

Investment planning     _____

Tax planning            _____

Estate planning         _____

Insurance planning      _____

Integrated Planning     _____

Other _____

2)      What are your areas of specialization? What qualifies you in this field?  _____
_____
_____

3)      a)      How long have you been offering financial planning advice to clients?

        _____  less than one year
        _____  one to five years
        _____  five to ten years
        _____  more than ten years

        b)      How many clients do you currently have?
        _____  less than ten clients
        _____  11 to 39
        _____  40 to 79
        _____  80+

4)      Briefly describe your work history:

_____

_____

_____

_____

5)      What are your educational qualifications? Give area of study.
Certificate          _____

Undergraduate        _____

Advanced Degree      _____

Other _____

6)      What financial planning designation(s) do you hold?
_____    Certified Financial Planner
_____    Certified Public Accountant
_____    Personal Financial Specialists
_____    Chartered Financial Consultant;
_____    other:_____

7)      What financial planning continuing education requirements
do you fulfill? (_____hours every_____)

8)      What licenses do you hold?
_____    Insurance              _____    Securities
_____    CPA                    _____    JD
_____    other:_____

9)      a)      Are you personally licensed or registered as an
Investment Advisor with the:
          _____ State(s)?        _____ Federal Government?

If no, why not? _____

        b)      Is your firm licensed or registered as an Investment
Advisor with the:
          _____ State(s)        _____ Federal Government?

If no, why not? _____

    c) Will you provide me with your disclosure document Form ADV or its state equivalent form?
       \_\_\_\_ Yes      \_\_\_\_ No

If no, why not? _____

10)    What services do you offer?

_____

_____

_____

_____

_____

_____

11)    Describe your approach to financial planning:

_____

_____

_____

12)   a)    Who will work with me on my plan?
Planner:_____
Associate(s):   _____

    b)    Will the same individuals review my financial situation?   \_\_\_\_ Yes    \_\_\_\_ No

If no, who will?_____

13)    How are you paid for your services?
\_\_\_\_ Fee                 \_\_\_\_ Commission
\_\_\_\_ Fee and Commission    \_\_\_\_ Salary
\_\_\_\_ other: _____

14)    What do you typically charge?

FEE: Hourly Rate $____ per hour
Flat fee (range) $_____ to $_____
_____ Percent of assets under management
COMMISSION: What is the approximate percentage of the investment or premium you receive on:
_____ stocks/bonds
_____ mutual funds
_____ annuities
_____ insurance products
_____ other: _____

15)  a)  Do you have a business affiliation with any company whose products or services you are recommending?

_____ Yes          _____ No

Explain: _____

_____

b)  Is any of your compensation based on product sales?

_____ Yes          _____ No

Explain: _____

_____

c)  Do professionals and sales agents to whom you may refer me send any business, fees or other benefits to you?

_____ Yes          _____ No

Explain: _____

_____

d)  Do you have an affiliation with a broker/dealer?

_____ Yes          _____ No

e)  Are you an owner of, or connected with, any other company whose services or products I will use?

_____ Yes          _____ No

Describe:_____

_____

16)　　Do you provide a written client engagement agreement?
　　　　　_____ Yes　　　　　　_____ No
If no, why not? _____

TO CHECK THE DISCIPLINARY HISTORY OF A FINANCIAL
PLANNER OR ADVISOR, CONTACT ONE OR MORE OF THE
FOLLOWING:

Certified Financial Planner Board of Standards: 888-CFP-MARK
National Association of Insurance Commissioners: 816-842-3600
National Association of Securities Dealers: 800-289-9999
National Fraud Exchange: 800-822-0416 (fee involved)
North American Securities Administrators Assn: 888-84-NASAA
Securities and Exchange Commission: 800-732-0330

# Orderly Affairs

## APPENDIX B:
## Additional Resources Which May Be Helpful

ANNUITIES

Annuitiesnet (www.Annuitiesnet.com) is a niche search engine exclusive to the variable annuity and investment industry. www.Annuitiesnet.com

BENEFITS FOR SENIORS

The National Council on Aging (www.BenefitscheckUp.org) helps senior citizens and their families take advantage of government benefit programs. Provides free, confidential screening to determine eligibility for programs.

CONSUMER INFORMATION

Better Business Bureau (www.bbb.org)
Run by Council of Better Business Bureaus - search indicator to specific topics, you can submit a complaint online and BBB will try to resolve it.

Consumer Protection Bureau (www.ftc.gov/consumer.htm)
Government-run site. Bureau does not solve disputes but will investigate fraud and sometimes pursues legal action.

Consumers Union (www.consumersunion.org)
Run by publishers of Consumer Reports magazine - information listed categorically plus links to paid-subscription site.

Consumer World (www.consumerworld.org)
A portal with links to consumer-assistance resources.

Lemon Law America (www.lemonlawamerica.com)
Run by consumer-affairs attorneys - lists state laws protecting consumers, offers direct access to lawyers willing to defend consumer rights.

## FINDING A PERSON, BUSINESS, PHONE #, ADDRESS

This website is like the Yellow Pages, but for the entire United States: www.AnyWho.com.

## IRAs

A Roth IRA website provides technical and planning information on Roth IRAs for both financial professionals and consumers: www.rothira.com.

## LONG-TERM CARE

Long-Term Care Quote (www.ltcq.net or 800-587-3279)
Free quotes on up to three policies.

## MORTGAGES AND PMI

If you have in the past had an FHA mortgage that you paid off, you may have been entitled to a refund of mortgage insurance (instead of PMI, you probably had mutual mortgage insurance - MMI; or mortgage insurance premium - MIP). If you did not receive this refund from your FHA-insured lender, contact the Department of Housing and Urban Development at 800-697-6967. To learn if HUD owes you an FHA refund, to go www.hud.gov/fha/comp/refunds on the internet, and enter your borrower's name and FHA case number.

## NURSING HOMES

To check on the record of a Medicaid-approved nursing home, the National Citizens' Coalition for Nursing Home Reform (www.nccnhr.org) can provide a referral to your state's long-term care ombudsman, who is an advocate for nursing home residents and helps evaluate facilities (telephone 202-332-2275).

To check a particular facility's record of complaints and violations of federal standards, go to ww.medicare.gov and click on "Nursing Home Compare".

The Centers for Medicare and Medicaid Services has a free publication, "Guide to Choosing a Nursing Home" - call (800) 633-4227, or check ElderCare Locator at www.eldercare.gov (telephone 800-677-1116).

PENSIONS

If you might be owed a pension benefit, the Pension Benefit Guaranty Corporation's (PBGC) pension search program can help: www.pbgc.gov/search.

SOCIAL SECURITY

The federal Social Security Administration provides information on benefits and payments, among other things: www.ssa.gov.

# Orderly Affairs

## APPENDIX C

For each of us, life hands you problems and opportunities; sometimes referred to as lemons or making lemonade! As you look back over your life, to this point, there are probably five to six major events, or decisions, you were forced to deal with that helped mold and shape the person you are today. The authors have found that the simple process of reflecting upon the key events in our past have helped us, and our clients, formulate a strategy toward creation of wealth.

We would like to guide you through a similar process. Examine the questions below and take some time to ponder your responses. Then answer the questions as honestly as you can. No one need ever see or know your answers but you may find that they can become even more powerful if you share them with a trusted advisor or friend. It is our belief that if we can see what has held us back (and what has propelled us forward), in the past, we are more likely to identify strategies that can help us overcome, in just a few months, hurdles we thought were impossible.

If you find this process to be difficult, don't give up. It is not always easy to reflect on trying or painful experiences of our past. Try, instead, to reflect on the positive experiences where you managed to overcome seemingly impossible odds and identify what it is you did that allowed you to succeed. Remember to always honor your successes by giving them due consideration. There is a great deal of learning to be found in them, just as there is in our setbacks.

If you are still struggling with this process after working with it on your own, we invite you to order our detailed Success Strategy Worksheet, available through our website (www.strategicasset.net).

We have seen remarkable results when the process, along with the principles presented in this book, are used correctly. We truly wish you great success in this process, and urge you to consult with a qualified advisor.

## What five major events have brought me to this point in my financial life?

1) _____

2) _____

3) _____

4) _____

5) _____

## What five major changes must I make to achieve financial success?

1) _____

2) _____

3) _____

4) _____

5) _____

# NOTES

# Orderly Affairs

## Orderly Affairs

# Orderly Affairs

**ORDERLY AFFAIRS**
**Pathways to Financial Freedom for Everyone**
by
William M. Upson, CLU, ChFC and Steven F. Klamm, Esq.

# ORDER FORM

Fax this form to: (925) 688-1327
Telephone:    Call 1-800-765-0561 x146 toll free.
                  Please have credit card ready.
e-mail: info@strategicasset.net
             postal orders:        St. Bernie's Press
                                  P.O. Box 5558
                                  Walnut Creek CA  94596

Please send me _____ copies at $24.95 (US) each plus $5.00 per book S/H (up to 5 books - for larger orders please call for shipping/handling fee)

Name: _____

Address: _____

_____

Telephone/e-mail address: _____

*Sales Tax: Please add 8.25% (California addresses only).

Payment: Check or Money Order (payable to St. Bernie's Press)
               PLEASE DO NOT SEND CASH
               Credit Card (Visa or MasterCard only)

__V  __M/C  #_____     expires: _____

authorized signature:_____

QUESTIONS?  Please call our toll-free number listed above.